THE
COMPLETE
ASSEMBLY
RESOURCE BOOK

A year of collective worship
for Catholic secondary schools

Mike Anderson, Martin Grace and Paul Heesome

First published in 2001 by
KEVIN MAYHEW LTD
Buxhall, Stowmarket
Suffolk IP14 3BW

Scripture quotations are from the Good News Bible published by The Bible Societies/HarperCollins Publishers Ltd, UK, © American Bible Society, 1966, 1971, 1976, 1992.

0 1 2 3 4 5 6 7 8 9

ISBN 1 84003 588 9
Catalogue No 1500370

'Advent Adventure' and 'Jesus – the Last Week' illustrated by Paul Heesome; other illustrations by Steve English.
Cover design by Jonathan Stroulger
Edited by Helen Elliot
Typeset by Margaret Lambeth

Printed in China

Contents

This resource pack is dedicated to the pupils and staff of St Cuthbert's RC High School, Berry's Lane, St Helens.

Thanks to all who whole-heartedly used these materials as the basis of their classroom and assembly prayer.

Special thanks to Jackie Cavanagh for help with music and display suggestions.

Extra-special thanks to our families for their unswerving support and encouragement.

Acknowledgements

The publishers wish to express their gratitude to the following for permission to include copyright material in this book:

Stainer & Bell Ltd, PO Box 110, Victoria House, 23 Gruneisen Road, London N3 1DZ, for the extract from *Lord of the Dance* by Sydney Carter, © 1963, Stainer & Bell Ltd.

Hodder & Stoughton Publishers, 338 Euston Road, London, NW1 3BH, for the prayer 'Goodness is stronger than evil' by Desmond Tutu.

Every effort has been made to trace the owners of copyright material and we hope that no copyright has been infringed. Pardon is sought and apology made if the contrary be the case, and a correction will be made in any reprint of this book.

Overview

By law, schools are legally obliged to provide a daily act of collective worship. Logistically this can be a big problem for teachers. Many non-specialists are given the task of leading prayers with their form during registration time – the available time stretching from just a couple of minutes to a sometimes quite uncomfortable 10 minutes. Understand-ably, there can be a lack of confidence to try things out which, coupled with other demands which leave little time for preparation of materials, can mean that prayer time is not the sort of experience that enriches either pupils or teachers.

Included is a full year's worth of resource materials for those charged with the awesome responsibility of leading young people in prayer on a daily basis.

- The materials have been tried and tested through the full age range of an 11-16 secondary school, but some resources would certainly be usable with older children in junior schools.

- The materials are based around themes such as 'Hollywood Films', 'Plays of Shakespeare' or 'The Gifts of the Spirit'.

- Within each theme (lasting from three to seven weeks) are materials for each week.

- The materials vary from theme to theme but include two minute introductions, short reflections, mini-biographies, scripture passages and reflections, and pupil activities of varying length – all of which can be adapted to individual circumstances.

- Each week has a photocopiable 'prayer of the week' for wall display.

- Materials can also be used as a resource for assembly providers.

- With each theme come suggestions for display and relevant music.

    In addition, there is an Advent Calendar project entitled 'Advent Adventure' and a Lenten Stations of the Cross project entitled 'Jesus – the Last Week', each with 15 posters and relevant 'thoughts for the day'.

A time for . . .

A seven-week series based on Ecclesiastes 3

A time for . . . PLANTING

INTRODUCTION

In Western society, the idea of planting a seed, tending it and eventually harvesting a crop has lost much of its meaning because we get so much food that is pre-packaged. People in other continents like Asia and Africa have a much better understanding of planting. They need to know which seeds to plant where, when to plant, how deep to plant, how far apart seeds should be planted and so on. Their lives depend on getting these things right. If they get them right and the weather is kind, then their seeds will develop and they will have what they need to live.

To a certain extent, our own lives depend on how we choose to develop our attitudes. Take the opportunity this week to think about the attitudes you would like to plant and develop – attitudes towards others, towards work, towards play and towards God.

ACTIVITY

Ask your pupils about the seeds they would like to sow in the world – they could be seeds which bring happiness, laughter, less suffering in the world, etc. Ask them to think about the seeds that they would like to plant in their own lives – maybe being more organised, hardworking, less easily offended, less likely to hurt others, more willing to put others first, and so on.

Ask pupils to write these down. It would be in keeping with the theme if they could write them down on small circles ('seeds'). Then collect them in and display them or keep them safe until later in the year when they can be looked at again to see if any of the 'seeds' have developed.

GOSPEL STORY (Mark 4:30-32)

Jesus said: **'The kingdom of heaven is like a mustard seed. Even though this is the smallest of all seeds, when it grows it is the biggest shrub of all and has such large branches that the birds come and take shelter in them.'**

In the English language we have many similes – as thin as a rake, as brave as a lion, as quiet as a mouse, for example. Can you think of any more? At the time of Jesus, there was a Jewish simile: 'as small as a mustard seed'. Jesus uses this to encourage his few followers not to be discouraged, because eventually their number would grow. In 1995, an estimated 33.2 per cent of the world's population were followers of Jesus. Jesus makes a difference to their lives. His Gospel values of love and justice and serving others make a difference in the world. Let's pray that these values will make a difference to us. Then we can make a difference in school, at home, in our communities and in the world.

SPECIAL PERSON

Rosa Parks was an ordinary black woman in 1960s America. One day, after she had finished work and then shopping for her family, she got on the bus home. She sat down, tired. The bus started to fill up and a white man went to Rosa, expecting her to stand up for him. (At the time, blacks were supposed to stand up so that whites could sit.) She stayed sitting and was arrested.

When the other members of the black community heard this, they decided they had to act. For a whole year, no black got on a bus until the bus company had lost so much money that they got rid of the rule that said whites were better than blacks. Imagine it, for a whole year, blacks walked long distances, to work, to the shops. They left home early in the morning and returned late at night. But they never gave up. Rosa Parks had planted a seed of non-violent resistance in them and this inspired their crusade for justice. A little-known minister was particularly inspired and he took up the leadership of their cause. You may not have heard of Rosa Parks, but you will probably know the name of this minister – Martin Luther King.

PRAYER

Lord, sometimes I feel bad about myself –
my self-esteem is as small as a mustard seed.
Sometimes, my love for others
is as small as a mustard seed.
Sometimes, my belief in you
is as small as a mustard seed.

Lord, help me to grow in self-esteem,
in love for others and in faith in you. Amen.

A time for ... HEALING

INTRODUCTION

Our bodies are amazing things. If we cut ourselves, or catch a cold, the body basically heals itself. We do have to go to the doctors sometimes; these days they can perform some fantastic procedures which were unthinkable only a few decades ago – things like transplants and micro-surgery.

There has also been a tremendous growth over the last few years in 'complementary medicine' – things like aromatherapy, herbalism and acupuncture.

However, doctors cannot help us heal the hurts we cause each other in our relationships. We can cause hurt by name-calling, by what we do and say, and by whom we exclude. This week, we are going to think about the healing of the spirit. We cannot very often heal our own hurts. We need others to help us do that. However, we can help heal the hurts we have caused others. This week, let's think about how we can heal others – how we can be spirit doctors – and ask God for the sensitivity and courage to be active healers.

ACTIVITY

If you have ever been in a dentist's waiting room, you will have experienced the 'delights' of *Readers' Digest*. One of the regular features is 'Laughter Is the Best Medicine'. Laughter is very good physiologically as well as psychologically. Why not, as part of your prayer time this week, have a laughter slot and give pupils a chance to share jokes? (A couple of minutes at afternoon registration might be a good time.) Why not run a 'caption competition' by taking in a photo and asking pupils to come up with a funny caption? The emphasis is on 'having a laugh' together. It's also a chance to talk with pupils about the difference between 'laughing with' and 'laughing at'.

You could close each session with the simple prayer:
Lord, thank you for laughter. Amen.

GOSPEL STORY (Mark 1:40-42)

A leper came to Jesus, knelt before him and said: 'If you want to – you can heal me.' Jesus felt sorry for the man and reached out and touched him saying, 'Of course I want to! Be healed!' And the leprosy left him at once and he was cured.

Leprosy is a terrible disease. A couple of years ago, Blue Peter ran an appeal to help sufferers who often lose the use of parts of their body as a result of leprosy. It is also a disease which disfigures. At the time of Jesus, lepers were treated as outcasts. They were not allowed to live in the villages and towns and had to stay away from people and ring bells and shout, 'unclean! unclean!' if they came near anyone, to warn them. They were de-humanised. The most significant part of this story is not that Jesus had the power to heal – but that Jesus reached out and touched him – treating him like a fellow human being.

In our society, we very often treat the mentally handicapped or the disabled badly. We might shy away from them or stare at them or use hurtful terms like 'spaz'. We might treat classmates as outcasts by talking about them behind their backs or excluding them from our groups. This week, make a special effort to reach out to others and not treat them as outcasts.

SPECIAL PERSON

Leonard Cheshire was born in 1917 in Cheshire. During World War II, he was a pilot in the famous Dam Busters Squadron and he won the Victoria Cross for bravery. In 1945, he was one of the British observers who witnessed the dropping of the atomic bomb on Nagasaki. The bomb killed 40,000 people.

After the war, Leonard tried a number of jobs. He tried to set up a home for ex-servicemen but it failed. His life was changed when a colleague, Arthur Dykes, who was dying from cancer, had no one to look after him. Leonard took him into his own home and was amazed at how Arthur's belief in God helped him through his pain and subsequent death. Eventually, Leonard himself became a Catholic and his new-found faith inspired him to open his home to others who were sick but had no one to look after them. This was the first Cheshire Home.

Leonard devoted his life to help those who were suffering and though he never gained any medical qualifications, he helped in the healing of many people's loneliness and helplessness. Leonard died in 1992, by which time there were 85 Cheshire Homes in the UK and 185 in 50 countries overseas.

PRAYER

Love beyond measure, mercy so free,
your endless resources, given to me,
strength to the weary, healing our lives,
your love beyond measure has opened my eyes. Amen.

A time for . . . BUILDING

INTRODUCTION

One of the first toys we get as children is a set of building bricks. Have you noticed, though, how much easier it is for a baby to knock over a tower that has been built than to actually build the tower? As the child grows older though, he or she gets more pleasure out of building houses or walls. The child moves on to Duplo or Lego and these bricks help them create their own world in which they can play for hours.

This week we are going to think about building and the choices we face in our relationships. Basically, we can be builders of **steps**, **walls** or **bridges**.

Builders of **steps** like to make themselves look more important than others. They like to get on their steps and look down on others.

Builders of **walls** like to keep some people or things close to them and to keep other people and things away from them. Builders of **walls** can be selfish in their relationships. While they might not think of themselves as superior to others, they do not feel they have much to learn from others – preferring to be left alone with what they are comfortable with within their walls.

Builders of **bridges** like to experience new ideas and want to reach out to others. Bridges are more difficult to build than either steps or walls, so builders of **bridges** need to be quite determined and resilient.

Christians are called to build the kingdom of God here and now. It is a kingdom of **bridges**. This week consider what you build.

ACTIVITY

The song for Comic Relief 1995 contained the following words:

'Love can build a bridge – between your heart and mine.
Love can build a bridge – don't you think it's time?
Don't you think it's time?'

Do a class brainstorm on people and issues which need a bridge to unite them (most effective if you have a bridge already drawn on a large piece of sugar paper).

Examples: Catholics and Protestants in Northern Ireland, the poor and the rich, those with jobs and those without jobs, parents and teenagers.

Finish with a simple prayer like:

Help us, Lord, to build bridges rather than steps and walls. Amen.

SPECIAL PERSON

About 10 years ago, an ordinary man became a hero because he built a very special bridge.

The *Herald of Free Enterprise* was a huge passenger ferry which crossed the Channel daily. One day, it left Zeebrugge and one of the crew failed to secure the bow doors. As a result, water flooded into the lower car-deck of the ship and it started to sink. Over 170 people died in this disaster, but it would have been more had it not been for this man who formed himself into a human bridge to allow other passengers to clamber to safety over him.

Fortunately we are not likely to be in such a position, but we can make the effort to build bridges to help other people around us.

PRAYER

Lord God, your creation shows me
how wonderful the world can be.
Jesus, your example shows me
how to make the world a better place.
Holy Spirit, give me the courage
to build the kingdom of God – here and now. Amen.

A time for . . . SILENCE

INTRODUCTION

Silence can be very special. After the Hillsborough disaster in 1989, thousands of people made a pilgrimage to Anfield to lay their scarves or flowers there in remembrance of those who had died. As they filed through the ground, they were silent. It was a special moment for anyone who experienced it.

On Armistice Day, two minutes silence is now kept again throughout the country in memory of those who died in two World Wars. Radio stations, supermarket tills and school classrooms fall silent.

In these cases, silence is a sign of respect, but silence can also be very awkward. It can be really embarrassing when you are with someone and realise you have nothing to say to them. It gets even worse when you try to think of something – only to find your mind has gone blank.

This week we are going to think about the right time to be silent. Sometimes things are better left unsaid. We often regret things we say in anger, on the spur of the moment – remember when Kevin Keegan lost his rag in an outburst against Alec Ferguson. And yet, sometimes we stay silent when we should speak up – we maintain a 'conspiracy of silence'.

We are going to ask God this week to help us in our decisions as to when to be silent and when not to be.

ACTIVITY

Hand out pieces of paper and ask pupils to reflect on 'Things I Wish I'd Never Said'. Times when they may have said things they regret might include:

- saying something hurtful to someone else;
- boasting about something or other;
- making an unkeepable promise.

When they have written them down, pupils could be asked to share what they've written. Then pupils could be given the opportunity to reflect in the following way:

So, let's think about why we regret saying these things. (pause)
Let's think about who ended up hurt. (pause)
Let's pray for that person, asking God to heal any hurt. (pause)
Let's think about any way in which we could put things right. (pause)
Let's ask God to help us put things right. (pause)

And now, let's get rid of these things we've said –
let's rip them up and throw them away –
and leave them behind us.

GOSPEL STORY (Matthew 6:1-4)

And Jesus said to them:

'Be careful not to parade your good deeds before others to attract their attention. If you do this, you will lose all reward from your Father in heaven. When you give money to help others, do not tell everyone about it. This is what the hypocrites do to win people's admiration. They have already received their reward. No, when you help someone, do not let your left hand know what your right hand is doing, and your Father in heaven – who sees all that is done in secret – will reward you.'

This is quite difficult to come to terms with. Most people want to help others, but it is also nice if other people notice and praise us for it. Why not do something for others this week and keep it to yourself?

SPECIAL PERSON

During World War II, a British girl called Odette Churchill was parachuted into France to help the Resistance Movement organise the escape of shot-down pilots.

Odette was captured by the Gestapo and suffered terrible torture, but she did not betray any member of the Resistance Movement. Even the brutal expertise of the Gestapo could not break her spirit. Odette survived the war and her story was made into a film.

It's a salutary lesson for us who are often only too willing to 'drop others in it'. Maybe today's challenge could be to hold our tongues, rather than use them at other people's expense.

PRAYER

God, give me the patience to hold my tongue
when I should be silent.
Give me the courage to speak out
when I should speak out.
But most of all, give me the wisdom
to know the difference. Amen.

A time for . . . CELEBRATING

INTRODUCTION

No doubt we can all remember the way we celebrated the dawn of the new millennium: parties, fireworks, cards and so on. There is no doubt that times have changed over the last hundred years, never mind the last two thousand years. For example:

The last century saw the invention of the aeroplane, television, personal computers, Walkman – the list goes on and on! All of these would have seemed miraculous to the people of the nineteenth century. What 'miraculous' innovations will this century bring?

What has not changed though, is the Christian's mission to be a living example of the message of Jesus, to build the kingdom of God according to the gospel values of love and justice. No doubt there have been many times when we have failed, but this week let's celebrate those things we have achieved!

ACTIVITY

We often use the term 'celebrity' to indicate that a person is well known. You'll be able to name plenty of celebrities yourself. However, a celebrity is someone whose life and achievements should be celebrated. And so – we are all celebrities! Today, let's celebrate our own gifts. Let's think about what we have brought to our school. It may be a sense of humour; it may be the gift of making friends; it may be the gift of not badmouthing others.

Have a class brainstorm on what gifts they bring between them. Then display it in your class. You can close by thanking God for the gift of each other and challenging the pupils to celebrate each other – to say something positive about someone else as often as possible.

GOSPEL STORY (Luke 15:3-7)

The Pharisees and teachers of the Law were criticising Jesus for being friendly with sinners so Jesus told them this parable:

'Suppose one of you has a hundred sheep and loses one of them – what do you do? You leave the other ninety-nine sheep in the wilderness and go looking for the one that got lost until you find it. When you find it, you are so happy that you put it on your shoulders and carry it back home. Then you call your friends and neighbours together and say to them, "I am so happy I found my lost sheep. Let us celebrate!"'

At the time of Jesus, shepherds were not regarded very highly. In fact, they were often the butt of jokes in the same way that these days the Irish are often unjustifiably ridiculed. Jesus actually describes a pretty strange situation. Surely the last thing you would do if you lost one sheep from among a hundred would be to leave the ninety-nine in the desert to wander off or be attacked by wolves? But, if you look at the story as an example of how much God loves us – it's very profound. God's love for those who wander off is so strong. Maybe you have drifted away from God's love or shut God out of your life. Maybe you don't feel good enough to try to develop a relationship with God. Nonsense! – God loves you and will welcome you back anytime. You're special! Celebrate your specialness and give yourself a chance to pray this week.

SPECIAL PERSON

Some years ago, our nation celebrated the release of Terry Waite, who was an adviser to the Anglican Archbishop of Canterbury. In 1981, Terry had helped to negotiate the release of some British hostages from Iran. In 1985, he managed to get Libya to release some British hostages. Each time, he put himself in considerable danger in order to prove to the hostage-takers that he was a man of integrity. However, in January 1987, while trying to negotiate the release of some hostages in Lebanon, he was himself taken prisoner. Terry spent over three years in a room two metres square, in solitary confinement. The only thing that got him through was his belief that God was watching over him. He was eventually released in November 1991.

He is an example of the tremendous strength that can be gained when we place our problems before God. The answers do come, although not necessarily as quickly as we want, nor in the way we expect them.

PRAYER

Lord, help me to smile and laugh
whate'er my mortal state.
Yes, even in life's darkest hour,
Lord, help me to celebrate. Amen.

A time for . . . DANCING

INTRODUCTION

This week our theme is 'A time for . . . DANCING'.

Dancing is a world-wide phenomenon. All cultures have dances which are part of their heritage. Dancing, though, has its fashions – some members of staff will remember the jive, the bump, and the dance to the Birdie Song! (Although they probably won't demonstrate them unless you ask politely!) American line dancing is popular at the moment and *Riverdance* and *Lord of the Dance* are enjoying worldwide success; ballroom dancing may soon become an Olympic event.

Dancing, whether stylised or improvised, expresses a personal response to music and reveals something about the dancer. The prevailing emotions expressed through dance are joy and love. Dancing is one way in which you can express the 'inner self'.

This week, we will be thinking about our 'inner selves' and how we, as humans, need to express our feelings and beliefs – not necessarily through dance, but through religion. Give yourself a chance this week to look for the good things in God's creation – in yourself and in other people – and 'dance your own dance' in response.

ACTIVITY

There are many types of dance. Ask pupils to brainstorm as many different dances as they can in two minutes. Each dance expresses emotion in a different way; ask pupils to decide which dance most closely fits in with their own personality (e.g. graceful like ballet, energetic like the jive, wanting to fit in with everyone else – line dancing).

Ask which dance most closely fits members of their family, and finally ask which dance most closely fits their idea of God. (Can they imagine God dancing at all?) Pupils can discuss in pairs, groups or as a class. Close with a short prayer like:

Lord, thank you for the joy of dance. Amen.

OLD TESTAMENT READING (ZEPHANIAH 3:14-17)

Sing and shout for joy, people of Israel! Rejoice with all your heart, Jerusalem! The Lord has ended your punishment; he has removed all your enemies. The Lord, the king of Israel, is with you; there is no reason now to be afraid.

The time is coming when they will say to Jerusalem, 'Do not be afraid, city of Zion! Do not let your hands hang limp! The Lord your God is with you; his power gives you victory. The Lord will take delight in you, and in his love he will give you new life. He will dance with shouts of joy over you as on a day of festival.'

When we think of God the Father it tends to be as a sort of Santa Claus figure in white robes, sitting on a throne looking down on us. However, this reading gives a very different picture indeed. God loves us through all our difficulties, and when we triumph God DANCES over us and SHOUTS for us. This should encourage us and remind us that – whether we are aware of it or not – God is always there for us. We are special – so special that our God (the God of the universe) – takes delight in our seemingly insignificant lives and DANCES with joy for us.

SPECIAL PERSON

You will all probably remember Roy Castle, the presenter of *Record Breakers*, who died of cancer a few years ago. He was an incredibly talented man – an accomplished musician and a brilliant tap-dancer.

What Roy Castle is remembered for, though, is the great fight he put up against cancer. He fought the disease for a number of years and confounded doctors with his resilience and cheerfulness. Before he died he said that he did not want people to be sad at his death, and at his own request a jazz band played at his memorial service.

Roy Castle has probably had more influence on people's lives because of the way he died than he ever did as a successful entertainer and presenter. His courage and zest for life in the most difficult situation make him a great role model.

PRAYER

Lord, you danced in the morning when the world was begun
and you danced in the moon and the stars and the sun.
You came down from heaven and you danced on the earth.
At Bethlehem you had your birth.
Lord, thank you! Amen.

A time for . . . LOOKING BACK

INTRODUCTION

One of the most popular tracks on the Oasis album *What's the Story (Morning Glory)* – one of the biggest selling records of the 1990s – is 'Don't Look Back in Anger'. Looking back – reviewing – reflecting – these are all perfectly natural human instincts. It's good to look back, but only if we do it in the right way.

Adults often look back through 'rose-coloured spectacles' and think everything was much better in the 'good old days'. And it's good to be sentimental about special times in our lives. Adults tend to be pretty selective about some of these memories though and, although they say the good old days were best, they are quite prepared to tell youngsters today how lucky they are. There's a famous sketch devised by the Monty Python team where some ageing self-made businessmen reflect on the terrible childhood they had, each trying to outdo the other in the awful- ness of it all. It culminates in one claiming he lived in a shoebox in the middle of the motorway, ate gravel because the family was so poor, and had to get up three hours before he went to bed, so he could go to work for an employer whom he had to pay for the privilege of having his limbs chopped off!

Looking back is a good thing to do, especially if we learn something from it. There are often times in our lives when things go horribly wrong and we just don't understand why. But some time later, we can see that at least something can be salvaged from the wreckage – even if it is only that we had the strength to get through it somehow. Often it is in the darkest moments that we experience God. This week, as we look back, let's try to find something good in what has happened this term so far.

ACTIVITY

WOW!

Ask pupils to reflect on 'wow!' moments in their lives. 'Wow!' moments are those times when you're left in awe by something or someone. It can be an ambition realised, a 'first' experience of something, a song, a moment when you felt completely fulfilled, a moment when you felt God was close.

Close with the simple prayer:
Lord, thank you for my special memories.
Amen.

SPECIAL PERSON

Just imagine it – you have been imprisoned for 26 years because you have campaigned against injustices in your country. For 26 years you are denied freedom. For 26 years you have to sleep in a cell while the people who put you there live in luxury. For 26 years you dream of being free and ending the injustices your people suffer.

Then, you are set free. Within five years you become the most powerful person in your nation. You have the chance to punish those who imprisoned you. What would you do? Would you imprison them? Have them expelled from your country? Would you enjoy seeing them suffer?

This happened to a man recently – and instead of looking back in anger and seeking to get his revenge, he decided on a policy of reconciliation. Even though many of his people wanted revenge, he counselled them against it. There are problems still but his country is a place of hope now – not hatred. It is a nation that is working for the future. The nation is South Africa – the Rainbow Nation. The man's name – Nelson Rolihlahla Mandela.

PRAYER

Lord, when I look back I feel I have let myself down.
Lord, when I look back I see people I have hurt.
Lord, when I look back I hear cruel words I have said.

Lord, help me to move forward, confident that you forgive me.
Amen.

A TIME FOR PLANTING

Lord, sometimes I feel bad about myself –
my self-esteem is as small as a mustard seed.

Sometimes, my love for others
is as small as a mustard seed.

Sometimes, my belief in you
is as small as a mustard seed.

Lord, help me to grow in self-esteem,
in love for others and in faith in you.

Amen.

A TIME FOR HEALING

Love beyond measure, mercy so free,

your endless resources, given to me,

strength to the weary, healing our lives,

your love beyond measure has opened my eyes.

Amen.

A TIME FOR BUILDING

Lord God, your creation shows me
how wonderful the world can be.

Jesus, your example shows me
how to make the world a better place.

Holy Spirit, give me the courage
to build the kingdom of God – here and now.

Amen.

A TIME FOR SILENCE

God, give me the patience to hold my tongue
when I should be silent.

Give me the courage to speak out
when I should speak out.

But most of all, give me the wisdom
to know the difference.

Amen.

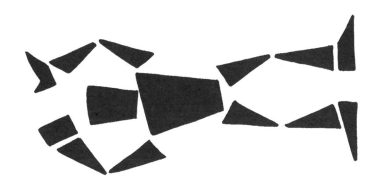

A TIME FOR CELEBRATING

Lord, help me to smile and laugh

whate'er my mortal state.

Yes, even in life's darkest hour,

Lord, help me celebrate.

Amen.

A TIME FOR DANCING

Lord, you danced in the morning when the world was begun

and you danced in the moon and the stars and the sun.

You came down from heaven and you danced on the earth.

At Bethlehem you had your birth.

Lord, thank you!

Amen.

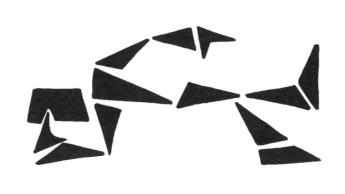

A TIME FOR LOOKING BACK

Lord, when I look back I feel I have let myself down.

Lord, when I look back I see people I have hurt.

Lord, when I look back I hear cruel words I have said.

Lord, help me to move forward,

confident that you forgive me.

Amen.

Display Idea for 'A time for . . .' Theme

Set aside an area in the room and bring in appropriate artefacts/symbols each week to develop the area (suggestions below).

Week 1   A time for . . . Planting

Picture of a tree, potted plant, garden tool, packet of seeds, gardening book.

Week 2   A time for . . . Healing

A selection of empty pill boxes, aromatherapy oils, bandages or first aid box.

Week 3   A time for . . . Building

A brick, pictures of constructions, a bridge. (You could even build your own wall or bridge using any materials which are available – straws, shoeboxes, Lego, Meccano sets.)

Week 4   A time for . . . Silence

A candle lit during prayer time and an open Bible.

Week 5   A time for . . . Celebrating

Balloons, decorations, streamers, tinsel, party music.

Week 6   A time for . . . Dancing

Ballet shoes, pictures from magazines.

Week 7   A time for . . . Looking Back

Diary, calendar, old greetings cards or letters, photographs, personal artefacts from pupils.

Suggested Songs/Music for 'A time for . . .' Theme

Week 1   A time for . . . Planting

'All good gifts' – from *Godspell*

Week 2   A time for . . . Healing

'Heal the world' – Michael Jackson
'Lay your hands' – Carey Landrey
'Healer of the sick' – Francesca Leftley, from *21st Century Folk Hymnal*/CD
'Deep within my heart' – Mike Anderson, from *Dance in Your Spirit*/CD

Week 3   A time for . . . Building

'Don't build your house' – Karen Lafferty, from *21st Century Folk Hymnal*/CD
'Love can build a bridge' – Comic Relief 1995

Week 4   A time for . . . Silence

'The sound of silence' – Simon and Garfunkel
'When you say nothing at all' – Ronan Keating

Week 5   A time for . . . Celebrating

'Come on and celebrate' – Patricia Morgan and Dave Bankhead, from
21st Century Folk Hymnal/CD
'Celebration time' – Kool and the Gang
'Sing alleluia' – Mike Anderson, from *Dance in Your Spirit*/CD

Week 6   A time for . . . Dancing

'Dance in your Spirit' – Mike Anderson, from *Dance in Your Spirit*/CD and
21st Century Folk Hymnal/CD

Week 7   A time for . . . Looking Back

'Don't look back in anger' – Oasis
'Yesterday' – The Beatles

The Gifts of the Spirit

A seven-week exploration

Wisdom

Introduction

Normally when it is someone's birthday, his or her family and friends give gifts which that person usually receives with delight. But, at Christmas, because Jesus is so special, all of us celebrate his birthday by giving and receiving gifts.

Mind you, we've all had gifts that we've not really used. You can probably think of some even as recently as last Christmas. Such gifts get stored away and may not reappear until you accidentally stumble over them during a clearout.

For the next seven weeks we are going to look at seven of the gifts of the Holy Spirit. These are gifts that sometimes we have without realising it. Over the seven weeks, we are going to look at ourselves, to see if we have really received these gifts and how we might be able to use them.

Daily Prayer

Lord, you know me so very well.
Help me to know myself better.
Help me to be wise in my words and actions.
With your help I can do it.

Amen.

Pause for thought

Wisdom is about making choices, and acting on those choices.

Here is an acronym to remind you about that:

What I Say Destroys Or Mends.

- Think about what you say this week.
- What will you do?
- Destroy or mend?

Activity   Here are some sayings about wisdom. Read them. Ask pupils which saying they think is the most important and useful, or get them to put them all into rank order. Then display the one chosen as most important somewhere in class for the rest of the week. You could perhaps ask a class member to write it on a larger piece of paper.

1   'It is the province of knowledge to speak, and it is the privilege of wisdom to listen.'

   Oliver Wendell Holmes (1809-94), US writer and physician.

2   'History teaches us that men and nations behave wisely once they have exhausted all other alternatives.'

   Abba Eban (b. 1915), Israeli politician. Speech, 16 Dec 1970, London.

3   'The stick and the reprimand give wisdom to children; if they have their own way, they will make their parents ashamed of them.'

   Proverbs 29:15, Hebrew Bible.

4   'Silence is as full of potential wisdom and wit as the unhewn marble of great sculpture.'

   Aldous Huxley (1894-1963), British author.

5   'Lord, grant me the courage to change the things I can change, the serenity to accept the things I can't change, and the wisdom to know the difference.'

   Traditional prayer

Scripture   Solomon was the son of David, the greatest Jewish King. When Solomon was quite young he took over as king and God told him that he would give him anything he wanted. Solomon thought about this and asked for the gift of wisdom. If God offered you *anything* you wanted, what would it be?

Anyway, one day Solomon was put to the test. Two women were brought before him. They both claimed a particular baby was theirs. Solomon pondered the problem, then ordered a soldier to cut the baby in two!

Immediately one of the women shouted out that she would rather the other woman have the child than see it cut in half. Solomon knew then that the woman who shouted out must have been the mother.

Solomon did rule wisely and perhaps his greatest achievement was the building of the Temple in Jerusalem, which stood for nearly a thousand years – probably considerably longer than the Millennium Dome will last, despite the technology and materials available to us!

Knowledge

Introduction

The song 'I know him so well' is from an Andrew Lloyd Webber musical and in the song two women are singing about the same man. They both sing that they know him so well, but actually they could be singing about different men, because one sings that all he needs is security while the other sings that what he really needs is his freedom. The irony is that really they don't know this man very well at all. They just know certain aspects of him well.

This is true about many of our relationships. We know things about a person rather than really knowing them. So how do we get to know a person? Through doing things with them, spending time with them, talking and listening to them, being with them in all sorts of situations.

What about doing some of these with Jesus this week? Have a few minutes of quiet each day. Try to picture Jesus by your side during the day. Think how he would deal with the situations you face. Talk to him in your mind. Read about him in the Gospel of Mark in a Gideon Bible, if you have one. Get to know him.

Daily Prayer

**Lord, you know me so very well.
Help me to get to know others better.
Help me to use what I know for good rather than bad.
With your help I can do it.**

Amen.

Pause for thought

'A little knowledge that acts is worth infinitely more than much knowledge that is idle.'

Kahlil Gibran, Lebanese poet

- Where do you stand on this?

- Are you good at putting ideas into action?

- Is there anything you know now that you should be doing something about?

37

Activity   Last week, one of the sayings that we discussed was:

'It is the province of knowledge to speak and the privilege of wisdom to listen.'

Here are some situations to think about and explore.

What more do you need to know?

How should you respond? (Try to get beyond the 'report it to a teacher' syndrome.)

1   You see an older pupil crying in the toilets.

2   You hear another pupil boasting that they have stolen something from a classroom.

3   You know that a friend of yours is having a difficult time at home financially. Now you hear some younger children calling them names because of their trainers.

4   You overhear a teacher talking about something personal.

5   You overhear a pupil talking about something personal.

6   You are out with a cousin of yours and are offered an 'E' for free.

Scripture   Everyone knows the story of Adam and Eve. So, answer these questions and let's see how much you know about one of the most famous pieces of literary history.

1   How did God make Adam?

2   How did God make Eve?

3   What were the two special trees in the Garden of Eden?

4   Who tempted Eve?

5   What did Eve eat that was forbidden?

6   What did Adam and Eve notice after this?

7   Who did Adam blame?

8   What happened to Adam and Eve?

Answers

1   God made Adam out of dust and then breathed into his nostrils.

2   While Adam was asleep, God took one of his ribs and covered it in flesh.

3   Tree of Life and Tree of Knowledge.

4   Serpent (note this was only a symbol of Satan – there is no mention of the devil in the text).

5   Fruit from the Tree of Knowledge (not an apple).

6   They were naked.

7   Adam blamed Eve.

8   They were expelled from the Garden of Eden – so they could not eat from the Tree of Life, which meant that one day they would die.

Awe and Wonder

Introduction

In our increasingly technological, digital and conspicuous consumer society, it is easy to become blasé about the world. For example, it is commonplace for people to fly to other countries. At the beginning of the last century, such an idea would have been inconceivable. It is now possible to communicate with people on the other side of the world by means of telephones and computers. Just a few decades ago this would have seemed ridiculous. Humans have even stood on the moon! All wonderful achievements!

And yet, truly wonderful moments may come not through technology but through other people. The first time you fall in love is wonderful. You can be filled with wonder when you see the miracle of a little baby. When someone achieves something in spite of terrible difficulties – you can be awestruck.

This week, try to focus on what is wonderful in the people around you. Each of us is a miracle – a wonder to be appreciated. Let's enjoy each other – every single one of us made in the image of God. (It makes you realise what a sense of humour God must have.) So, go on, look in the mirror each morning this week and say to yourself – 'I am the pinnacle of God's creative power! I'm awesome!'

Daily Prayer

Lord, you know me so very well.
Help me to appreciate myself.
Help me to appreciate the wonder of everyone I meet.
With your help I can do it.

Amen.

Pause for Thought

'What is this life if, full of care,
we have no time to stand and stare?'

William Davies (1871-1940)

Davies was an interesting character who left the UK on a cattle ship to hitch-hike through America. He had to have a leg amputated after he jumped off a train in Canada. He returned to England and slept rough, making his living as a street singer. His poem 'Leisure' was voted fourteenth in the 'Nation's Favourite Poems' poll on National Poetry Day, 1995.

Activity

The Seven Wonders of the Ancient World were:

- the Pyramids
- the Hanging Gardens of Babylon
- the Mausoleum at Halicarnassus
- the Temple to the goddess Artemis at Ephesus
- the Colossus of Rhodes
- the Statue of Zeus by Phidias
- the Pharos (lighthouse) at Alexandria.

All of them were made by humans, using their God-given talents. Only the Pyramids of the above remain.

Try to come up with your own list of seven modern wonders of the world. (Don't limit this to buildings. You can include any human achievement over the last century, e.g. going to the moon, breaking the speed of sound, discovery of penicillin, etc.)

Then try to come up with seven natural wonders of the world. (You can include mountains, rivers, animals, insects, etc.)

Finally try to make a list of your seven human wonders of the world. (These should be the seven people you think are most wonderful, whether famous or seemingly ordinary.)

Scripture

O Lord, our Lord, your greatness is seen in all the world! When I look at the sky, which you have made, at the moon and the stars, which you set in their places – compared to them, what are human beings, that you think of them and care for them?

Yet you appointed them rulers over everything you made; you placed them over all creation: sheep and cattle, and the wild animals too; the birds and the fish and the creatures in the seas.

Psalm 8

Nowadays, telescopes and satellites can reveal the most accurate and amazing information about the stars. Astronomers tell us that some stars we see simply don't exist anymore; that – because they are so far away – we see them as they were millions of years ago. It takes the light from them that long to travel to us (even at 186,000 miles per second!)

The words of the Psalm above – originally a song written possibly by King David – express the writer's wonder at the stars and moon. Although written 3,000 years ago, the words still mean something today. We do have a responsibility to the world, to the environment, to the animals and to each other. Have a look at the stars this week – realise how vast the universe is. Be mindful of your place in it.

Understanding

Introduction

During this theme we have been looking at the gifts of the Holy Spirit. So far, we've thought about Wisdom, Knowledge, and Awe and Wonder. The next gift is that of Understanding. So many of the problems in the world today are caused by lack of understanding – problems on a global scale, like the debt crisis facing many poor nations; problems on a much more personal level – perhaps between classmates and work colleagues. Maybe you've had an experience like this when you feel that someone just doesn't understand you and yet makes judgements which affect you.

Of course, understanding is very much a two-way process, which underlines the importance of communication. We can't expect people to understand us if we don't take opportunities to express ourselves. Mind you, neither can we absolve ourselves of the responsibility to listen to others. Too often, we can be so busy expressing how we feel that we don't listen carefully enough to others. Have you ever been in a conversation or argument when, as soon as you've said something, you start formulating what you are going to say next – rather than listen to what the other person is saying?

This week, the challenge is to make a more conscious effort to listen and understand.

Daily Prayer

Lord, you know me so very well.
Help me to understand my own feelings and those of others.
Help me to understand how you want me to live my life.
With your help I can make a difference.

Amen.

Pause for Thought

'If you don't understand yourself you don't understand anybody else.'

Nikki Giovanni (1971), American poet.

- Do you sometimes do things – then wonder why you did them?
- Do you sometimes say things – that you wish you hadn't said?
- Do you sometimes wish you understood yourself more?

If you answer 'YES' to these questions – welcome to the human race!

Activity

Here is a list of anagrams. Each word fits in the blank in the following sentence.

.... **experiences can develop our understanding.**

1	SUUUALN	(Unusual)
2	ENW	(New)
3	FREDENTIF	(Different)
4	TENXCIGI	(Exciting)
5	SHERGREFIN	(Refreshing)
6	ASD	(Sad)
7	STINGET	(Testing)
8	RATSICIT	(Artistic)
9	VAINGEET	(Negative)
10.	SEVERID	(Diverse)
11	GRISTEENTIN	(Interesting)
12	RACEYNESS	(Necessary)
13	GIGLUNERL	(Gruelling)

Try and work them out. The initial letters of the first words spell an appropriate word. Comprende?

Scripture

I want you to be happy, always happy in the Lord; I repeat, what I want is your happiness. Be tolerant with everyone – the Lord is very near. There is no need to worry; but if there is anything you need, pray for it – and that peace of God, which is so much greater than we can understand, will guard your hearts and thoughts.

St. Paul's Letter to the Philippians 4:4-7

St. Paul wrote this letter about 25 years after the death of Jesus. This was before any of the Gospels were written and, at the time, Paul was under arrest for telling people about Jesus. In another part of this letter, Paul warns the early followers of Jesus that certain enemies are out to get them. He also wrote about two of the followers of Jesus who were at each other's throats, begging them to come to some agreement. It seems these were troubled times. But what was Paul's advice? He said there was no need to worry and that prayer was the answer; that prayer would bring peace, a peace beyond human understanding!

Maybe some of his words apply to you today. Certainly, it is good to hear that we should be looking for happiness in our lives. So often, people think religion is about rules and regulations which restrict freedom and impose discipline. On the contrary – whatever we live our lives by should bring us happiness, contentment and fun!

Courage

Introduction

There is a common misconception that brave people feel no fear. This is ridiculous. After all, if you are not frightened of something, you have no need to be brave.

Modern-day Christians have a great heritage of courage: from Jesus himself, to the early martyrs and the persecuted Catholics of the Reformation, right up to this century and people like Maximilian Kolbe and Oscar Romero.

Fortunately, the number of people called to such amazingly courageous acts of faith are few, but we are all called to take courage in our own situation: in school, at home, in society; to stand up and be counted as witnesses to Jesus. For example, do you have the courage to stand up for those who are given a hard time by bullies who intimidate, ridicule and humiliate? Courage costs, because you can end up a victim too! But maybe your example will make the difference and turn the tide against those who seek to make life a misery for others.

Daily Prayer

Lord, you know me so very well.
Help me to cope with fear – fear of being left out,
fear of being laughed at, fear of disappointing others.
Help me to have the courage to do what is right –
even if it is unpopular.
With your help I can do it.

Amen.

Pause for Thought

'I'm very brave generally, only today I happen to have a headache.'

Tweedledum in *Alice Through the Looking Glass* by Lewis Carroll

- Can you relate to this?

- What do you use as excuses for wimping out when you should show courage?

- Is there some area of your life in which you need to take courage?

Ask God to help!

Activity   *Arachnophobia* was a pretty scary film about deadly spiders invading a town in America. A 'phobia' is an irrational fear of something. Here are some – can you find out what they are?

CLAUSTROPHOBIA	(fear of enclosed spaces)
ASTRAPHOBIA	(fear of lightning)
TRISKAIDEKAPHOBIA	(fear of the number 13)
POGONOPHOBIA	(fear of beards)
NYCTOPHOBIA	(fear of the night)
XENOPHOBIA	(fear of foreigners)
CAINOTOPHOBIA	(fear of anything new)
ZOOPHOBIA	(fear of animals)
AILUROPHOBIA	(fear of cats)
MONOPHOBIA	(fear of being alone)

One of the ways to overcome these phobias is 'aversion therapy'. For instance, arachnophobics will go through small steps leading up to actually holding a spider. It can be very successful.

Are there any small steps you could take to overcoming your fears?

Scripture   *Between three and six o'clock in the morning Jesus came to the disciples, walking on the water. When they saw him walking on the water, they were terrified. 'It's a ghost!' they said, and screamed with fear. Jesus spoke to them at once. 'Courage!' he said. 'It is I. Don't be afraid!'*

Then Peter spoke up: 'Lord, if it is really you, order me to come out on the water to you.'

'Come!' answered Jesus. So Peter got out of the boat and started walking on the water to Jesus. But when he noticed the strong wind, he was afraid and started to sink down in the water. 'Save me, Lord!' he cried.

Matthew 14

In this story, we see how Peter has the courage to leave the relative safety of the boat. But there is more to this than meets the eye. Water is generally used in our society as a symbol of cleanliness and goodness, because it is essential for life. However, at the time of Jesus water had two meanings: one was 'goodness', the other 'evil', because at various points in their history, the Jews had had crops destroyed by floods.

So, the story of Jesus walking on the water symbolises Jesus' power over evil and we, like Peter, are called to take courage in the battle against the evil in our own world. So, take courage and be confident that Jesus will help you just as he helped Peter.

Right Judgement

Introduction

The gift we are looking at this week is Right Judgement. In 1999, at the Brit Awards, Robbie Williams was judged by members of the music industry to be Best Male Artist, to have sung the Best Single – 'Angels' – and to have been in the Best Video – Millennium. For each of these he received a statuette. Maybe you thought that someone else should have won one or more of these awards, but, like it or not, the records show that, according to the music industry, Robbie Williams won.

You see the thing that makes a judgement different from an everyday choice is that a judgement has an air of finality about it. In the case of the Brit Awards the judgements from previous years can be looked up. They are a snapshot in time of particular judgements – they cannot be changed.

When a defendant in court is judged, that judgement is a formal declaration of guilt or innocence after all the evidence available has been considered. Our justice system allows people to appeal against judgements but eventually the opportunities to appeal run out and a final judgement is made.

This week, we are thinking about the gift of right judgement. We need to ask ourselves how we make judgements about other people. Do we judge them on the basis of lots of evidence or do we judge them merely on what others say about them? Do we really get to know them before we sentence them by the way we treat them? Do we consider and look for their good points as well as what we believe to be their bad points? Maybe you've been misjudged in the past. Try to remember how it felt and use that to help you in judging others fairly.

Daily Prayer

Lord, you know me so very well.
Help me to judge others fairly.
Help me to look for good in others.
Help me to reserve judgement rather than condemn.
With your help I can do it.
Amen.

Pause for Thought

'I have a dream today that one day my children will live in a nation where they will not be judged by the colour of their skin but by the content of their character.'
Martin Luther King (1929-68)

- Do you judge by the colour of skin?
- What is your stereotype of Chinese people?
- What is your stereotype of black people?
- What is your stereotype of Pakistani people?
- Do you have prejudices?
- What is your stereotype of white people?

Activity

Make your own judgements as a class about the following categories:

- Best single (ever!)
- Best pop group (ever!)
- Person most likely to make England's football team into world champions
- Person most likely to make the world a better place
- Best role model for young men
- Best role model for young women
- Best maxim for life
- Most important event in human history

Why not compare them to the judgements of some of the other classes in school?

Scripture

Do not judge others, so that God will not judge you, for God will judge you in the same way as you judge others, and he will apply to you the same rules you apply to others.

Why, then, do you look at the speck in your brother's eye, and pay no attention to the log in your own eye? How dare you say to your brother, 'Please, let me take that speck out of your eye,' when you have a log in your own eye? You hypocrite! First take the log out of your own eye, and then you will be able to see clearly to take the speck out of your brother's eye.

Matthew 7:1-5

This forms part of the Sermon on the Mount – a collection of Jesus' teachings – which contains much humour. Look at the passage above and try to imagine how Jesus might have said it.

He uses this image of someone with a plank in his eye trying to get a speck of dust out of someone else's eye. Can you picture the absurdity of it? In other parts of the Sermon on the Mount Jesus exaggerates in order to make a point – but there is always a point!

In this case, Jesus is basically reiterating part of the prayer that he taught his followers. Can you work out which line?

Reverence

Introduction

The final gift of the Holy Spirit that we are considering in this series is Reverence. This is about treating God, ourselves and others with honour or respect. Reverence is very much part of our culture and tradition in this country.

Our judicial system has a formal way of expressing reverence – we address the judge as 'Your Honour'. In the House of Commons, members of Parliament address each other as 'The Right Honourable Member' – although they very often proceed to treat each other with less than respect. Our priests are formally addressed as 'Reverend' – as in The Revd Father . . . In church, Catholics genuflect as a sign of reverence towards God. In school, pupils show respect by addressing their teachers appropriately.

But reverence is not something to be afforded just to a select few – judges, MPs, clergy or teachers. No, reverence is about treating everyone with respect and treating everyone as if they matter to us. Jesus was quite revolutionary in this regard. His story is full of instances where he treats outcasts with respect. So, this week, let's try to walk in his footsteps and respect others. That's not to say we have to bow to people, but we can show reverence by listening to others. We can show reverence by not belittling others because they are different. We can show reverence by appreciating that they are just as important to God as we are.

Daily Prayer

Lord, you know me so very well.
Help me to appreciate this world.
Help me to honour those who care for me.
Help me to respect others even when I find them difficult.
With your help I can do it.

Amen.

Pause for thought

'We have not the reverent feeling for the rainbow that a savage has, because we know how it is made.'
Mark Twain (1835-1910)

- Can you enjoy the beauty of a rainbow?
- Does music touch your emotions?
- Can you look at the moon and still be impressed?

Or are you so sophisticated that you find no joy in them?

47

Activity

Last week, we made judgements about various categories. Here are just a selection of answers given by pupils in another school in 1999. Can you respect their judgements? Reverence is about accepting and valuing others' viewpoints, whether we agree with them or not.

- Best single (ever!): nominations included 'Millennium', 'Baby One More Time', 'Angels', 'Feed The World', 'Bohemian Rhapsody', 'Believe'.

- Best pop group (ever!): nominations included Steps, Oasis, The Beatles, and Five.

- Person most likely to make England's football team into world champions: nominations included Kevin Keegan, Terry Venables and Michael Owen.

- Person most likely to make the world a better place: nominations included Tony Blair, each one of us, Martin Luther King, Princess Diana, Michael Jackson, Muhammad Ali.

- Best role model for young men: nominations included Michael Owen, Cane, Johnny Vaughan and Winnie the Pooh. (The class who nominated Winnie the Pooh reckoned he was always cheerful, always took care of others – especially Piglet – and was pretty unmaterialistic, because the only thing he wanted was honey!)

- Best role model for young women: nominations included Princess Diana, Celine Dion, Mother Teresa, Billie, Britney Spears, Madonna, girls' mums.

- Most important event in human history: nominations included the end of World War II and the birth of Jesus.

Scripture

Jesus was having a meal in Levi's house. A large number of tax collectors and other outcasts were following Jesus, and many of them joined him and his disciples at the table. Some teachers of the Law, who were Pharisees, saw that Jesus was eating with these outcasts and tax collectors, so they asked his disciples, 'Why does he eat with such people?' Jesus heard them and answered, 'People who are well do not need a doctor, but only those who are sick. I have not come to call respectable people, but outcasts.'

Mark 2:15-18

Jesus respected everyone. He touched lepers – the outcasts of society in those days. (Maybe sometimes you feel left out by others.) He loved the disabled. (Maybe sometimes you feel disabled or inadequate in some way.) He spoke up for sinners. (Maybe sometimes you choose to do wrong.) Jesus seemed to be able to appreciate everyone as an individual. He treated them with respect and they loved him. He loves us too, even though we might not deserve it. So, we're called to follow the example of Jesus. Not easy? Certainly! Inconvenient? Definitely! Desirable? Absolutely!

Wissdom

Prayer

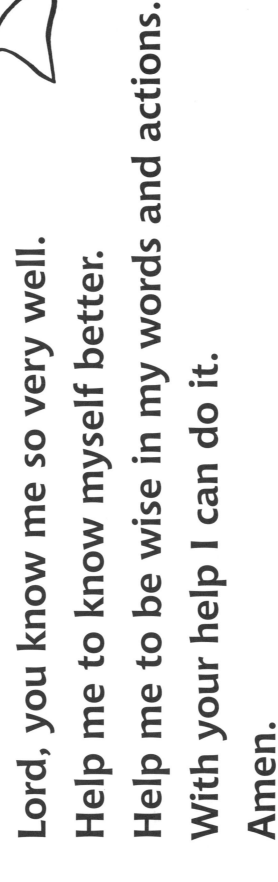

Lord, you know me so very well.

Help me to know myself better.

Help me to be wise in my words and actions.

With your help I can do it.

Amen.

Prayer

Lord, you know me so very well.

Help me to get to know others better.

Help me to use what I know for good rather than bad.

With your help I can do it.

Amen.

Knowledge

Prayer

Lord, you know me so very well.

Help me to appreciate myself.

Help me to appreciate the wonder

of everyone I meet.

With your help I can do it.

Amen.

Awe and Wonder

Prayer

Lord, you know me so very very well.

Help me to understand my own feelings

and those of others.

Help me to understand how you want me to live my life.

With your help I can make a difference.

Amen.

Understanding

Prayer

Lord, you know me so very well.

Help me to cope with fear –

fear of being left out,

fear of being laughed at,

fear of disappointing others.

Help me to have the courage to do what is right –

even if it is unpopular.

With your help I can do it.

Amen.

Courage

Prayer

Lord, you know me so very well.

Help me to judge others fairly.

Help me to look for good in others.

Help me to reserve judgement

rather than condemn.

With your help I can do it.

Amen.

Right Judgement

Prayer

Lord, you know me so very very well.

Help me to appreciate this world.

Help me to honour those who care for me.

Help me to respect others

even when I find them difficult.

With your help I can do it.

Amen.

Reverence

Display Idea for 'Gifts of the Spirit' Theme

A good central image for display would be a dove or cross from around which the prayer for each week is displayed.

Gifts of the Spirit

Suggested Songs/Music for 'Gifts of the Spirit' Theme

Week 1: Wisdom

'Never forget' – Take That

'Father and son' – Boyzone or Cat Stevens

Week 2: Knowledge

'I know him so well' – Elaine Page and Barbara Dickson

'Now I know what love is' – Mike Anderson, from *Dance in Your Spirit*/CD and *21st Century Folk Hymnal*/CD

Week 3: Awe and Wonder

'What a wonderful world' – Louis Armstrong or Alison Moyet

'Shine, Jesus, shine' – Graham Kendrick, from *21st Century Folk Hymnal*/CD

'Lord of life' – Mike Anderson, from *Dance in Your Spirit*/CD and *21st Century Folk Hymnal*

'Your love's greater' – Mike Anderson, from *Dance in Your Spirit*/CD and *21st Century Folk Hymnal*

Week 4: Understanding

'We can work it out' – The Beatles

'Some day we'll know' – New Radicals

Week 5: Courage

'When the going gets tough' – Boyzone

Week 6: Right Judgement

'The kingdom of heaven' – Mike Anderson, from *Dance in Your Spirit*/CD and *21st Century Folk Hymnal*/CD

Week 7: Reverence

'Be still, for the presence of the Lord' – David J. Evans, from *21st Century Folk Hymnal*/CD

'Heaven from here' – Robbie Williams

HOLLYWOOD FILMS

A four-week series

Week 1: Forrest Gump

Week 2: Gone with the Wind

Week 3: The Wizard of Oz

Week 4: Star Wars

'Prayer of the Week' Posters

Display Ideas

Suggested Songs/Music

FORREST GUMP

Introduction

Over the next four weeks we are going to be following a series on films during Sacred Time. We'll also be looking at the lives of some saints! But the film for this week is *Forrest Gump*.

This Oscar-winning film follows the life of Forrest Gump – someone who was not overly blessed in the brains department – and his encounters with famous people and events in recent history. He meets up with and influences Elvis. He fights in the Vietnam War, becoming a hero. He loves and nurses his childhood sweetheart, Jenny.

Although a simpleton, Forrest is a truly good man who responds positively to every situation he faces, and somehow discovers that he has the gifts and strength of character to help him come through the bad times.

We can all learn from his positive attitude to life.

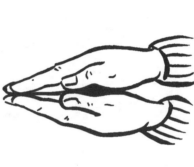

Famous Words

*'Life is like a box of chocolates –
you never know what you're going to get!'*

Sometimes in life we get surprises and sometimes shocks!

Reflect on your own life and think about times when you got a lovely surprise. Share these moments with others in your class.

Daily Prayer

Lord God,

help us to see the good in others;

help us to speak words which encourage;

help us to smile more.

Amen.

Saint of the Week

St Andrew

Andrew had a famous brother – St Peter. They were both fishermen. Andrew was with Peter when Jesus started to collect a band of followers (disciples), who left their homes in order to follow Jesus.

Andrew does not get much of a mention in the Gospels whereas Peter is very high profile. Perhaps Andrew was a bit jealous of Peter when Peter was appointed leader of the disciples. We don't really know, but if you've got brothers and sisters, maybe you've experienced what is called 'sibling rivalry'!

Anyway, Church tradition has it that Andrew visited Scotland after the death and resurrection of Jesus to tell people all about him. It is also believed that, during the early persecutions of the Church in the Roman Empire, Andrew was crucified but his cross was two pieces of wood arranged diagonally as opposed to vertical and horizontal.

As a result, Scotland – which claims Andrew as its patron saint – has as its flag a white diagonal cross on a blue background! And that in turn has become part of the Union Jack. Next time you see either of these flags, think about our connection with Jesus thanks to St Andrew.

Activity

Getting a box of chocolates is a treat. Giving someone a box of chocolates is a symbol of affection and love.

1 Think about your three favourite chocolates. You could do a class survey.

2 Now, imagine life is like a box of chocolates. The chocolates are all surprises which would make life better for the person you give them to. Think of someone special in your life and think about the three surprises you would like them to have if you could arrange it. For example, you might want them to have good health; you might want them to have the chance to visit someone; you might want them to have success in a job.

3 Now, think about the three surprises you would like yourself – but don't just think about money and what that can bring. There are other far more important things which can make your life happier.

4 Finally, if you were a chocolate, what do think you would be?

• Are you quite hard of heart on the inside but all sweetness and light on the outside – a hazelnut swirl?

• Do you make life difficult for others – a toffee chew?

• Do you try to be hard on the outside, but really you're quite gentle and soft on the inside – a chocolate eclair?

• What kind of chocolate would your friends be?

Gone With The Wind

HOLLYWOOD

Introduction

Gone with the Wind is an amazing movie. It was the biggest and most successful movie of its time.

Based on the novel by Margaret Mitchell, it follows the life of Scarlett O'Hara, a beautiful but manipulative girl, through the years before, during and after the American Civil War.

Scarlett had everything in life that some people regard as essential to happiness – wealth, looks and influence. However, Scarlett was one of those people who are rarely happy with what they have. Maybe you know someone like that.

Eventually, she lost the man she loved – Rhett Butler – but she refused to be crushed and downhearted. While we might not share her values, we can still admire her spirit.

Famous Words

'After all, tomorrow is another day!'

At the end of the film Scarlett O'Hara speaks these words. Sometimes it's easy to dwell on what has happened in the past and it can be hard to put the bad things behind us.

Reflect on your life – do you live in the past? If you do, take courage – don't forget about the past, but don't let it stop you being the best you can be.

Daily Prayer

Lord God,

help us to see that we can't change what has happened;

help us to see how we can put things right for the future;

help us to be the best we can be.

Amen.

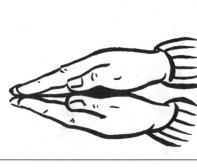

Saint of the Week

St Barbara

The story of St Barbara reads like a fairy tale!

Supposedly born in the fourth century, she is thought to have lived in Rome or Turkey during the reign of the Emperor Maximian.

Her father did not want her to marry so he built a tower and kept her there in solitude. However, while in her tower, she converted to Christianity, which at the time was punishable by death.

Her father took her to the Roman governor who had Barbara tortured, expecting her to give up her faith in Jesus and pledge allegiance to the Roman Emperor. But Barbara did not give in and her father took her to the top of a hill and chopped her head off. At that moment, Barbara's father was struck by lightning and died.

St Barbara thus became associated with praying during storms and is also the patron saint of artillery!

Activity

The famous last words of Scarlett O'Hara can help us focus on tomorrow. Have a go at writing a poem, each line of which starts with the letters in the word **TOMORROW.**

For example:

Truthful
Open
Mediating
Organised
Responsible
Reasonable
One day can make a difference
When will I be what I can be?

or

Trusting
Others?
Many times I've done that
Only to be
Rejected and hurt.
Running away isn't the answer
Only I don't want to be hurt again.
Will I ever trust someone else again? Maybe!

THE WIZARD OF OZ

Introduction

The *Wizard of Oz* was released in 1939 and starred Judy Garland. It was the first major studio film released in colour!

It's really the story of four characters each looking for something different. Dorothy is looking for the Wizard of Oz, who can take her back to her home town – Kansas – from which she has been taken by a twister!

On her journey on the Yellow Brick Road to the Emerald City, she meets the Scarecrow, the Tin Man and the Cowardly Lion. They each decide they will accompany her so that they can ask the Wizard to help them. The Scarecrow wants a brain, the Tin Man wants a heart and the Cowardly Lion wants some courage!

They have many adventures together and eventually realise that each of them already has what they were looking for. They just didn't realise how gifted they were because they hadn't used these gifts before.

This week, let's think about our own God-given gifts – some of which may be under-used!

Famous Words

'If I only had a . . .'

The Scarecrow kept saying, 'If I only had a brain!' The Tin Man kept saying, 'If I only had a heart!' The Cowardly Lion kept saying, 'If I only had some courage!'

What would the *'If only I had . . .'* be in your life as regards:

   (a) material things   (b) personal qualities

Do you have control over either of these?

Are you happy with what you have got and what you are?

Daily Prayer

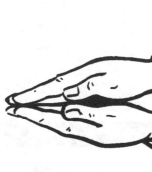

Lord God,

help us to see that we are all gifted;

help us to use our gifts;

help us to encourage others to use their gifts.

    Amen.

Saint of the Week

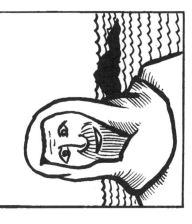

St Cuthbert

Cuthbert was born about AD 630, quite probably in Scotland. As a boy he was a shepherd but legend has it that he had an experience of God – a vision – which changed his life.

He went on to be a great scholar. At the age of 21, he became a monk and later helped to set up a monastery in Ripon. He was a bit of a rebel and was expelled from there when he and his monks refused to accept certain orders from the Church leaders in far distant Rome!

After a spell back in Melrose, Cuthbert went to Lindisfarne (also called Holy Island) where he was in charge for 12 years. He then spent eight years living alone on the nearby Farne Island from which he returned rather reluctantly to be Bishop of Hexham.

After three years as bishop he returned to Farne Island where he died shortly after. His body now lies in Durham Cathedral and his feast day is 20 March.

So there you are: St Cuthbert – a rebel, an academic, a leader, yet a man who longed for a simple life of prayer in natural surroundings.

Activity

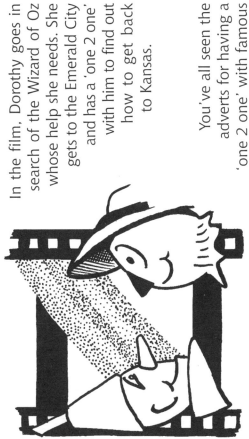

In the film, Dorothy goes in search of the Wizard of Oz whose help she needs. She gets to the Emerald City and has a 'one 2 one' with him to find out how to get back to Kansas.

You've all seen the adverts for having a 'one 2 one' with famous people, such as Ian Wright and Chris Evans. with Martin Luther King and Chris Evans.

Who would you like to have a 'one 2 one' with, and why? If you could only ask them three questions, what would they be?

Now, imagine having a 'one 2 one' with Jesus. What three questions would you ask?

Share your ideas with others near you or role-play the 'one 2 one' with someone taking on the roles of Jesus and your other heroes.

HOLLYWOOD STAR WARS

Introduction

Recently the first episode of *Star Wars* was released, somewhat strangely after episodes 4, 5 and 6!

When you strip the *Star Wars* saga of all the special effects, what you get is basically a story of an ongoing battle between good and evil. In episode 4, Obi-wan Kenobi is good and Darth Vader is the personification of all that is evil.

The same sort of struggles have been going on throughout the world for thousands of years. Unfortunately, people like Darth Vader have and do exist. You need only consider the Holocaust, in which six million Jews were exterminated, to realise this is true.

However, let's not lose sight of the fact that there is so much good in the world, too. Most people do choose good rather than evil most of the time and sometimes there are heroic examples of this – like Maximilian Kolbe, the priest who gave his life to save another's in the Holocaust. This week, let's try be more aware of the choices we face, and make good ones!

Famous Words

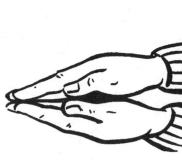

'The force be with you!'

These were the words spoken by Obi-wan Kenobi, which Luke Skywalker remembered when he needed help.

Can you remember any words that people have spoken to you which you remember particularly well?

Has anyone ever said just the right thing for you at just the right time?

Is it just possible that God helped them to say these words?

Daily Prayer

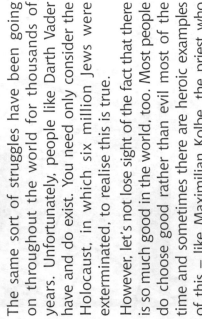

Lord Jesus,
**you promised you would always be with us.
Help us to be more aware of your presence**
in our lives.
Amen.

Saint of the Week

St Dominic

Dominic was born in Spain in 1170 into a reasonably wealthy family. He received a good education and went to university at the age of 17. He became renowned for his generosity and sold all his possessions to help the poor during a famine in 1191.

In the early 1200s he travelled to Rome and, on his return journey, was horrified by the way some priests were teaching the people things which Dominic regarded as wrong!

Dominic got together a group of priests and they studied, prayed and taught people more traditional views. He became heavily involved in education and believed it to be a vital part of the development of the individual. He set up an order – the Dominicans – some of whom travelled to England, Scandinavia and Germany, telling people about Jesus.

He died in 1221 and his feast day is 8 August.

Activity

'The force be with you!' are words spoken by Jedi knights. They are the words which inspire Luke to continue his struggle even when all seems lost.

Here are some other famous words. See if you can match them with the people below.

1 'I couldn't help it. I can resist everything except temptation.'
2 'You see but do not observe.'
3 'If I have seen further it is by standing on the shoulders of giants!'
4 'Come to me all you who labour and are heavily burdened. I will give you rest.'
5 'Love is blind.'

a Jesus
b Oscar Wilde (playwright and wit)
c Isaac Newton (scientist)
d Sherlock Holmes (fictional detective created by Sir Arthur Conan Doyle)
e William Shakespeare (playwright)

Answers: 1b, 2d, 3c, 4a, 5e

Talk about what each means. Which do you like best? If there were a phrase that you could be remembered for, what would it be?

The words of Jesus are recorded in the Gospels. Make a list of some of the sayings of Jesus that you can remember.

FORREST GUMP

HOLLYWOOD

Famous Words

'Life is like a box of chocolates – you never know what you're going to get!'

Daily Prayer

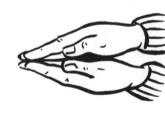

Lord God,

help us to see

the good in others;

help us to speak words

which encourage;

help us to smile more.

Amen.

GONE WITH THE WIND

HOLLYWOOD

Famous Words

'After all, tomorrow is another day!'

Daily Prayer

Lord God,

help us to see that we can't change what has happened;

help us to see how we can put things right for the future;

help us to be the best we can be.

Amen.

The Wizard of Oz

Famous Words

'If I only had a . . .'

Daily Prayer

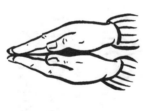

Lord God,

help us to see that we are all gifted;

help us to use our gifts;

help us to encourage others to use their gifts.

Amen.

STAR WARS

Famous Words

'The force be with you!'

Daily Prayer

Lord Jesus,
you promised you would
always be with us.
Help us to be more aware
of your presence in our
lives.
Amen.

Display Idea for 'Hollywood Films' Theme

Display the 'Daily Prayer' and 'Famous Words' sheets in the beams of drawings of spot/laser lights or on images of clapperboards.

Suggested Songs/Music for 'Hollywood Films' Theme

Week 1: Forrest Gump

'Around the world' – Nat King Cole

'Never forget' – Take That

'I'll be there for you' – The Rembrandts (Theme from *Friends*)

Week 2: Gone with the Wind

'Brand new start' – Paul Weller

'Could we start again, please?' – from *Jesus Christ Superstar*

Week 3: The Wizard of Oz

'Somewhere over the rainbow' – Judy Garland

'When the going gets tough' – Boyzone

'At every end there's a beginning' – Gladys Knight and the Pips

Week 4: Star Wars

Star Wars theme by John Williams

'Never forget' – Take That

'When you wish upon a star' – from *Pinocchio*

Plays of Shakespeare

A *four-week series*

Week 1: Much Ado About Nothing

Week 2: The Tempest

Week 3: Romeo and Juliet

Week 4: A Midsummer Night's Dream

'Prayer of the Week' Posters

Display Ideas

Suggested Songs/Music

Much Ado About Nothing

Introduction

One of the most successful films of recent years has been *Shakespeare In Love*. Over the next four weeks we will be looking at some of the titles of his plays, starting with *Much Ado About Nothing*.

This is a comedy in which the two main characters – Beatrice and Benedick – spend most of the time bickering and badmouthing each other. Eventually they realise that they actually love each other and they form an unlikely alliance to help another couple get married. Finally, after various trials and tribulations, there is a happy ending and everyone realises that their earlier difficulties are not that significant after all.

How true that is for us! We do sometimes face major problems in our lives. However insurmountable many of today's problems might seem, we will be able to look back in the years ahead and realise they were 'much ado about nothing'.

Daily Prayer

Lord – help me to accept the things I can't change.
Lord – give me the courage to change the things I can change.
And, above all, Lord –
give me the wisdom to know the difference.

Amen.

From Bard to Verse

'I do love nothing in the world so well as you:
is that not strange?'

Benedick to Beatrice in Act 4, Scene 1

Isn't it strange too that Jesus loves each of us?

No matter what we do!

No matter what we say!

No matter if we try to shut him out of our lives!

In fact, Jesus loves us so much that he opened his arms to hug us and we nailed them to a cross.

Activity

Here is a list of things that affect our lives in some way. Rewrite the list in rank order of their importance to you. (Most important at the top!) Then rewrite them in the order you think Bill Gates (the world's richest man) might place them. Finally, rewrite them in the order that Jesus might put them.

Being fashionable

Being rich

Being happy

Being generous

Being popular

Being successful

Being respected

Being loved

Compare the lists. If they are different, why are they different?

Scripture

Jesus said to them:

Why worry about clothes? Look how the wild flowers grow: they do not work or make clothes for themselves. But I tell you that not even King Solomon with all his wealth had clothes as beautiful as one of these flowers.

So do not worry about tomorrow; it will have enough worries of its own. There is no need to add to the troubles each day brings.

Matthew 6:28-29, 34

Do you get worried about clothes? Maybe you think or say things like:

- I could do with another pair of trainers
- That Nike jacket is last year's style
- I need a new Helly-Hansen
- I can't wear that – it isn't in fashion
- My mates'll laugh at me

Look at a TV news item about refugees or victims of natural disasters! Do you think they're bothered by such ideas?

If you're going to worry – worry about important things!

The Tempest

Introduction

This week's play starts with a shipwreck. One of the survivors is Ferdinand, a good-looking prince, who is washed up on an island inhabited by Prospero and his beautiful daughter Miranda.

The inevitable happens and the two young people fall in love. However, Prospero puts obstacles in their way. There are other storms along the way as Prospero, the rightful Duke of Milan, encounters his brother who usurped him. There is a plot against the life of Ferdinand's father, the King of Naples; and Caliban (Prospero's slave) and some drunken sailors try to get the better of Prospero.

However, the heroes survive the stormy goings on and they all live happily ever after. This week, let's consider the storms in our lives and maybe how we cause storms for other people.

Daily Prayer

**Just as you calmed the wind
and walked upon the sea,
conquer, my living Lord,
the storms that threaten me.**

Amen.

From Bard to Verse

*'How many goodly creatures are there here!
How beauteous mankind is!
O brave new world, that hath such people in't.'*

Miranda in Act 5, Scene 1.

Who are the *goodly creatures* in your life?

- the people who make you happy?
- the people who help you overcome your storms?
- the people who make you feel loved and valued?

Enjoy such people! Enjoy this brave new world that has so much good in it! Do your bit towards making it even better!

Activity

In Act 1, Scene 2, Ferdinand, who has just survived the shipwreck, wanders about the island and he hears a beautiful song, sung by the fairy, Ariel. Ferdinand says:

This music crept by me upon the waters,
allaying both their fury, and my passion, with its sweet air.

You've probably got some songs that soothe you and help you to stay calm. Talk about them and come up with a list of all-time 'soothers'. Then choose the three most soothing – the three most likely to keep you calm in times of trouble.

Here are a few to start you off:

- 'Perfect day' (various artists)
- 'Bridge over troubled waters' – Simon and Garfunkel
- 'I'll be there for you' – The Rembrandts (theme from *Friends*)
- 'Do not be afraid' (hymn)

Why not bring one in sometime this week and play it in prayer time?

Scripture

Suddenly a strong wind blew up, and the waves began to spill over into the boat, so that it was about to sink. Jesus was in the back of the boat, asleep. The disciples woke him up and said, 'Teacher, don't you care that we are about to die?' Jesus stood up and commanded the wind, 'Be quiet!' and he said to the waves, 'Be still!' The wind died down, and there was a great calm.

Then Jesus said to his disciples, 'Why are you frightened? Have you still no faith?' But they were terribly afraid and said to one another, 'Who is this man?'

Mark 4:36-41

This is a great story but isn't it strange that:

- Jesus managed to stay asleep in the midst of this tempest
- Jesus asked the disciples why they were frightened (wasn't it obvious?)
- Jesus told the disciples off for their lack of faith
- by the end of the story the disciples are more frightened than ever!

The question they asked remains relevant for us: *Who is this man, Jesus?* What does he mean to us?

Romeo and Juliet

Introduction

This is one of the most famous pieces of world literature. Its very title is so ingrained in our culture that to mention it evokes images of love. Even those who have neither seen nor read the play know that Romeo and Juliet were lovers.

Just a few years ago, a film was made of the play, starring none other than Leonardo Di Caprio. The opening of the film powerfully brings the story to life as members of the enemy households – the Montagues and Capulets – fight it out at a petrol station!

Amidst the anger, antagonism and hatred, Romeo and Juliet fall in love. However, their plan to live happily ever after ends tragically. An important letter is undelivered, misunderstanding ensues, and Romeo and Juliet both die. Yet their warring families come together in their grief and make a fresh start with each other. Love conquers all!

Daily Prayer

Put love in our hearts, Lord Jesus:
love for you, love for those around us,
love for those we find it hard to like.

Amen.

From Bard to Verse

'Seal up the mouth of outrage for a while,
till we can clear these ambiguities.'

Escalus, the Prince of Verona, in Act 5, Scene 3

(These words are spoken to members of the warring families upon their discovery of the dead couple.)

- Do you ever need to seal your mouth?
- Have you ever hurt someone by what you've said?
- Have you ever made things worse in a relationship by what you've said?
- Have you ever 'opened you mouth and put your foot in it', as it were?

Activity

There used to be a cartoon series in the daily papers entitled: 'Love is . . .' It portrayed two characters and the way they showed their love for each other in a sometimes very down-to-earth way. For example: 'Love is . . . doing the washing up while there are still clean plates in the cupboard' or 'Love is . . . giving her flowers just because you love her'.

Here is a series of statements about love:

Love is patient and kind;
it is not jealous or conceited or proud;
love is not ill-mannered or selfish or irritable;
love does not keep a record of wrongs;
love is not happy with evil, but is happy with the truth.
Love never gives up.

So how good are you at love – real love; not romantic, slushy love, but real down-to-earth love? Here is the same passage as before – but instead of 'love' the word 'I' is inserted. Count up as this is read; just how many of these phrases describe you? There are 12 in all:

I am (1) patient and (2) kind;
I am (3) not jealous, (4) not conceited, and (5) not proud;
I am (6) not ill-mannered, (7) not selfish, and (8) not irritable;
I (9) don't keep a record of wrongs;
I am (10) not happy with evil, but I am (11) happy with the truth.
I (12) never give up.

Ratings:
10-12 = very good   7-9 = average   1-6 = room for improvement

Scripture

Jesus said to them: 'My children, I shall not be with you very much longer. And now I give you a new commandment: love one another. As I have loved you, so you must love one another. If you have love for one another, then everyone will know that you are my disciples.'

John 13:33-35

At the Last Supper, Jesus gave his friends this new commandment. Not only does it replace the Ten Commandments, it also does away with the need for any other laws! Every other law could be done away with if everyone in the world could follow this one commandment to 'love one another'.

Maybe you can think of some laws that we just wouldn't need if everyone did love one another?

A Midsummer Night's Dream

Introduction

This is a fabulous play. It's got intrigue, love, comedy, a play within a play, magic potions, fairies, a wedding – and a happy ending!

In short, Theseus loves Hippolyta and Hippolyta loves Theseus. They are getting married – simple! Oberon loves Titania but they have a pretty on-off kind of relationship and it's more off than on for most of the play. Meanwhile Helena fancies Demetrius but Demetrius fancies Hermia. Lysander also fancies Hermia and fortunately for Lysander – Hermia fancies him and not Demetrius. Nobody fancies Helena – aah!

Confused? This is just the start! It makes *Eastenders* seem like *Postman Pat*. Eventually, though, everyone's dream comes true! This week we think about our dreams and how we can turn them into reality.

Daily Prayer

**Lord, the kingdom of heaven is a place
where there are no more tears,
no more pain and no more suffering.
Help us to work towards making this vision a reality
here and now.**

Amen.

From Bard to Verse

'The course of true love never did run smooth.'

Lysander (who fancies Hermia, remember?), Act 1, Scene 1.

Turning your dreams into reality is not something that necessarily comes easily. You have to work at it!

- Do you have the 'stickability' and determination to make your dreams a reality?
- Will you let disappointments put you off?
- Do you ever help others to make their dreams into reality?

Activity

Martin Luther King once said:

'I have a dream today that one day my children will live in a nation where they will not be judged by the colour of their skin but by the content of their character.'

You can look it up on most computer encyclopaedias and listen to the speech. It's very emotional.

What are your dreams for this nation and this world?

Work together to draft your own paragraph which starts:

'We have a dream today that one day our children will live in a *nation* . . .'

Now draft a paragraph that starts:

'We have a dream today that one day our children will live in a *world* . . .'

Issues you might like to consider are war, ethnic cleansing, starvation, world debt, injustice, torture.

Scripture

A man suffering from leprosy came to Jesus, knelt down, and begged him for help. 'If you want to,' he said, 'you can make me clean.'

Jesus was filled with pity, and stretched out his hand and touched him. 'I do want to,' he answered. 'Be clean!' At once the disease left the man, and he was clean.

Mark 1:40-42

In this week's play a magic potion is used on various characters as they sleep. When they wake the potion makes them love the first person they see – sometimes with hilarious results.

Jesus, however, did not need a magic potion to love people. Even the wretched leper who would have been disfigured, smelly and pretty unattractive was loved by Jesus.

The amazing thing in this story is not that Jesus healed the leper. The amazing thing is that he reached out to touch the leper. It's a challenge to us to reach out to those who feel left out in our school, our families and our society.

Prayer

Lord – help me to accept the things I can't change.

Lord – give me the courage to change the things I can change.

And, above all, Lord – give me the wisdom to know the difference.

Amen.

The Tempest

Prayer

Just as you calmed the wind

and walked upon the sea,

conquer, my living Lord,

the storms that threaten me.

Amen.

Prayer

Put love in our hearts,
Lord Jesus:

love for you,

love for those around us,

love for those we find it hard
to like.

Amen.

Prayer

Lord, the kingdom of heaven is a place where there are no more tears, no more pain and no more suffering.

Help us to work towards making this vision a reality here and now.

Amen.

Display Idea for 'Plays of Shakespeare' Theme

Focal point – large picture of the bard himself!

Week 1: *Much Ado About Nothing*

Display adverts for clothes and possessions on one side of the display area. On the other side, display pictures of refugees and/or images of poverty.

Week 2: *The Tempest*

Display extracts of letters to problem pages (things which cause turmoil) from teen magazines.

Week 3: *Romeo and Juliet*

Under the title 'Love One Another', display either a large heart or cross in which pupils can write practical ways they can show love and concern for others.

Week 4: *A Midsummer Night's Dream*

Under the title 'Our Dreams', display either a large thought bubble or a series of smaller thought bubbles in which pupils can write their dreams.

Suggested Songs/Music for 'Plays of Shakespeare' Theme

Week 1: *Much Ado About Nothing*

'No matter what' – Boyzone

'All I once held dear' – Graham Kendrick, from *21st Century Folk Hymnal*/CD

Week 2: *The Tempest*

'Bridge over troubled water' – Simon and Garfunkel

'I will be with you' – Gerard Markland, from *Songs of the Spirit, Liturgical Hymns Old and New*.

'Calm me, Lord' – David Adams and Margaret Rizza, from *21st Century Folk Hymnal*/CD

Week 3: *Romeo and Juliet*

'Love is all around me' – Wet, Wet, Wet

'Love is all you need' – The Beatles

'Flying without wings' – Westlife

Week 4: *A Midsummer Night's Dream*

'Dream' – The Everly Brothers

'Heaven help us all' – Wet, Wet, Wet

Caring for My Neighbour

A four-week series based on Church social teaching

WEEK 1: Option for the Poor

WEEK 2: Equal in Dignity

WEEK 3: All Human Life Is Sacred

WEEK 4: The Common Good

'Prayer of the Week' Posters

Display Ideas

Suggested Songs/Music

Option for the poor

INTRODUCTION

Every day, we make choices – about what we wear; about what we say; about what we eat; about who we are going to spend time with; about what we are going to do. In fact, it could be argued that life is all about making choices – about seeing what options are available and then taking one of them.

This week, we are focusing on the incredibly difficult challenge that followers of Jesus face – the challenge always to take an option for the poor.

We all take this option from time to time – but do we do it often enough? When was the last time you took an option that would benefit the poor? Maybe it was on Comic Relief Day; maybe it was by buying *The Big Issue* in town from one of the homeless; maybe it was by giving some money to the charity collectors outside your local supermarket. Whenever it was – do you think it was enough?

Nobody expects you to change the world, but you can remember the poor as you pray. Maybe, this week, you could pray for the chance to take an option for the poor. Any money you raise won't change the world, but it will make a difference to someone somewhere.

Can your class take an option for the poor?

ACTIVITY

Ask pupils what they are going to have to eat today. Make a list on the board.

Then ask them to work in groups to decide who has been involved in bringing certain items from the field to the table. They could draw a chain – each link being someone involved in the process.

The idea is to remind us that many people are involved in enabling us to eat and for that we should be thankful. Many people today will not eat and we are incredibly lucky to have so much.

Why not say a prayer before you go for dinner this week? This simple grace before meals suffices.

**For what we are about to receive
may the Lord make us truly thankful.**

Amen.

GOSPEL STORY (Matthew 25:31-46)

One of the great parables is about how on Judgement Day we will be separated just as a shepherd separates the sheep and goats. Some will go to heaven – others will hear Jesus say to them:

'I was hungry but you would not feed me, thirsty but you would not give me a drink; I was a stranger but you would not welcome me in your homes, naked but you would not clothe me; I was sick and in prison but you did not take care of me.'

Then they will ask him: 'When, Lord, did we ever see you like this – hungry or thirsty or a stranger or naked or sick or in prison – and did not help you?'

And Jesus will reply, 'I tell you, whenever you refused to help my poor brothers and sisters – you refused to help me.'

These, then, will be sent off to eternal punishment, but the righteous will go to eternal life.

Which group will you be in?
* Do you treat everyone as if they were Jesus?
* Do you take an option for the poor or an option for yourself?
* Do you do something about it – even if only in a very small way?

PRAYER

Brother Jesus – you were born poor;
you fed the hungry;
you loved the outcasts.
Help me to find a way to take an option for the poor.
Amen.

WEEK 2 OF 4

Equal in Dignity

INTRODUCTION

Most supermarkets and producers these days are keen to promote their products as being environmentally friendly and recyclable. But in some countries there are children who are professional recyclers. This sounds rather grand until you consider children like 10-year-old Shireen from India. Shireen scavenges on a city waste tip. If she sells waste paper and plastic bags worth 18p, she will have enough to buy lunch; if not, she goes hungry.

Children like Shireen exist all over the world – in Zaire, they are known as 'sparrows'; in Peru, they are known as 'fruitbirds'. Wherever they are, as they trample through the rubbish heaps, they run the risk of catching all sorts of skin infections and diseases.

When they get older, they often turn to prostitution as it is considered a better alternative.

In Brazil, vigilantes and policemen have murdered tens of thousands of these street kids because they are considered to be a blight on society.

And yet, these are children. They are worthy of love. They deserve to be treated as being equal in dignity. It is only by accident of birth that they live in squalor and we live in comfort.

This week we are challenged to think about how we regard others.
* Do you consider yourself to be superior to others?
* Do you treat others as if you were superior?
* Do you oppress others by what you say to them or by how you look at them?
* How would you treat Shireen – dirty and smelly, uneducated and desperate?

ACTIVITY

The Scripture passage is about everyone being equal in dignity. Ask the class to think of groups of people who are discriminated against – who are not treated as equals. Then construct a charter for equality along the following lines:

We believe that the following are
equal in dignity:
blacks and whites,
Christians and Muslims,
Catholics and Protestants,
rich and poor, etc.

NEW TESTAMENT WRITING (Galatians 3:28)

If you believe in Jesus there can be no difference between Jews and Gentiles, between slaves and free people, between men and women. We are all one in union with Christ Jesus.

This was written by St Paul about 25 years after the death of Jesus. It was part of a letter sent by Paul to a group of Christians living in what we now call Northern Turkey.

It seems that they were having a few problems in accepting that anyone could be a Christian. Paul is quite clear that everyone is to be treated as being *equal in dignity*. What he wrote is amazing if you consider the kind of society Paul lived in. To suggest women should be treated as equals was subversive and revolutionary. Nowadays, we have no problem with equality for the sexes. However, believe it or not, it was only 22 years ago that Britain formally accepted than men and women were equal in dignity. So what Paul wrote was centuries, if not millennia, ahead of its time.

PRAYER

Made in your image – male and female.
Made in your image – black and white.
Made in your image – strong and weak.
Made in your image.
Amen.

WEEK 3 OF 4   **All Human Life Is Sacred**

INTRODUCTION

Each November, the country looks back and remembers the millions who died in the wars of the last century. This week we reflect on the Catholic Church's teaching that all human life is sacred.

The actual word 'sacred' means 'worthy of respect'. So, the Catholic Church teaches that all humans are to be respected and treated accordingly. If you asked 100 people if they believed that all human life is sacred you would expect them all to agree, because this idea is such a fundamental aspect of all human societies. People would agree from Paris to Prague; from St Helen's to St Lucia; from Acapulco to Zanzibar. And yet, there are times when we value one person's life above another; there are times when certain groups in society are not deemed to live worthwhile lives; there are times when nations will treat human lives as if they don't matter.

You know that millions died in the two world wars, but did you know that more human lives have been lost because of abortions than in those wars? The most vulnerable form of human life – the unborn foetus – has been massacred. And yet it hardly makes the news. Is that because the victims have no voice to speak out?

In November we keep a minute's silence for those who died. Why not have a minute's silence this week as we think of those who cry a 'silent scream' as they die.

ACTIVITY

Here are some facts about the development of the unborn child in the womb. Simply ask pupils to guess when the different stages of development occur.

When . . .

does the heart start beating?	*25 days*
do the legs and arms begin to form?	*4 weeks*
do bones appear?	*6 weeks*
do fingers and thumbs start forming?	*7 weeks*
do kidneys and other organs form?	*10 weeks*
are the vocal chords formed?	*12 weeks*
does the baby reach half its birth length?	*16 weeks*
do eyebrows and eyelashes start forming?	*20 weeks*

When can abortions be legally carried out?
Up until the twenty-second week of pregnancy – when the unborn baby has all the above indicators of being human.

Finish with a simple prayer:
>	Thank you, Lord,
>	for the precious gift of human life.
>	Amen.

OLD TESTAMENT READING (Exodus 20:13)

Do not commit murder.

What a stark reminder to us all. This is one of the Ten Commandments. Notice how it doesn't describe any circumstances in which it is OK to kill.

Over the centuries people seem to have added certain phrases for themselves to make this commandment seem to read:
>	Thou shalt not kill unless someone attacks you first – or
>	Thou shalt not kill unless the person is a Jew – or
>	Thou shalt not kill unless the person is a murderer – and so on.

Some people would argue that it is possible to justify the killing of a fellow human. For example, would it have been justifiable to kill Hitler?

Whichever way you look at it, if this commandment was kept by all, we would have a very different world.

PRAYER

Creator God – the unborn children are yours.
The disabled and infirm are yours.
Everyone in the world is yours.

And Lord, I am yours – help me to make a difference.
Amen.

WEEK 4 OF 4 The Common Good

INTRODUCTION

During November, we remember especially those who lost their lives in armed conflict during the last century. This week, we are going to think about why they were willing to make the sacrifice they did. We can't be sure of the exact reasons but it is not unreasonable to assume that they felt they were defending their country and all the people in it – especially their loved ones. They were willing to take the risk of dying in the cause of the Common Good – in other words, they did not fight purely for themselves, they fought because the nation as a whole would benefit.

We too can make less dramatic sacrifices in the cause of the Common Good. Dropping a piece of litter is probably easier for us to do than finding a litter bin, but if we all choose to drop litter, we all suffer. We suffer because we have to trudge through litter and because we have to live in the knowledge that some of our school community do not care about the others in it – the other pupils, staff, cleaners, caretakers, visitors, etc. This is just one example of how small acts of selfishness affect the Common Good in our school.

However, if we think about how our actions affect others and respond accordingly, each of us can play a part in promoting the Common Good in our families, school, neighbourhoods, nation and world.

ACTIVITY

Discuss with pupils how one or each of the following affects the development of the Common Good within their school. A brief example is given.

Graffiti
- affects those who are named – they feel unhappy, their unhappiness is reflected in their attitudes towards others
- affects all who see it – they may think badly of the named person, they may feel they have to laugh about it with others even though they know it's wrong
- affects those who have to clean it up – they may think badly about every individual in the school as they can't be sure who wrote it

- inhibits the development of the Common Good because relationships are damaged.

Calling people names and gossiping about them

Seeing people being disrespectful towards prefects and doing nothing about it

Lying about why homework has not been done

Telling parents only one side of an incident in school.

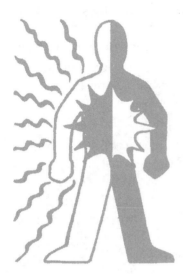

NEW TESTAMENT READING
(from **John 6:5-9**)

And Jesus said to them. 'How much food do you have?' Andrew, who was Simon Peter's brother, said, 'There is a boy here who has five loaves of barley bread and two fish. But they will certainly not be enough for all these people.'

This is taken from that famous story of the Feeding of the Five Thousand. No one knows what really happened but this little extract suggests that Andrew – one of the first disciples – has gone to the trouble of finding some food, but stopped once he had found enough for Jesus and the other apostles. Perhaps he was expecting Jesus to send all the people away so they could get on with their own picnic.

After all, what was the point of being apostles if you never got to be with Jesus by yourselves? They were probably fed up with being followed by crowds and having to be glorified 'bouncers' who protected Jesus. Andrew was not thinking of the Common Good of the 5,000 men and their families who were there. As you know, Jesus took what had been found and transformed it, so that everyone was satisfied. In the same way, Jesus challenges us to see beyond our own needs and seek the Common Good.

PRAYER

Lord, help us to realise that *all human life is sacred*;

that we are all *equal in dignity*;

that we are called to take an *option for the poor*;

that we should try to act in the cause of the *Common Good*.

Amen.

Option for the Poor

Brother Jesus – you were born poor;

you fed the hungry;

you loved the outcasts.

Help me to find a way

to take an option for the poor.

Amen.

Equal In Dignity

Made in your image – male and female.

Made in your image – black and white.

Made in your image – strong and weak.

Made in your image.

Amen.

All Human Life Is Sacred

Creator God –
the unborn children are yours.

The disabled and infirm are yours.

Everyone in the world is yours.

And Lord, I am yours –
help me to make a difference.

Amen.

The Common Good

Lord, help us to realise

that **all human life is sacred**;

that we are all **equal in dignity**;

that we are called

to take an **option for the poor**;

that we should try to act

in the cause of the **Common Good**.

Amen.

Display Idea for 'Caring for My Neighbour' Theme

Set aside some wall space for these four weeks and build up
a display around the focal point of a globe.

WEEK 1: Option for the Poor

Selection of CAFOD, Christian Aid and Oxfam posters, perhaps with a selection of 'Traidcraft' goods.

WEEK 2: Equal in Dignity

Collage of newspaper/magazine cuttings illustrating inequality in the world.

WEEK 3: All Human Life Is Sacred

Display information from this week's activity, perhaps with information about the Samaritans.

WEEK 4: The Common Good

Newspaper cuttings and magazine extracts about environmental issues.

Relevant Songs/Music for 'Caring for My Neighbour' Theme

Week 1: Option for the Poor

'Feed the world' – Band Aid

'Dancing with the missing' – Sting

'Another day for you and me in Paradise' – Phil Collins

Week 2: Equal in Dignity

'He ain't heavy – he's my brother' – The Hollies

'As long as you love me' – Backstreet Boys

'One love' – Bob Marley

Week 3: All Human Life Is Sacred

'Papa don't preach' – Madonna

'Wonder child' – Mary Black

Week 4: The Common Good

'World in union' – The Rugby Union World Cup Theme

'A brand new start' – Paul Weller

'Larger than life' – Backstreet Boys

'One' – U2

A FOUR-WEEK SERIES BASED ON

GREEK MYTHOLOGY

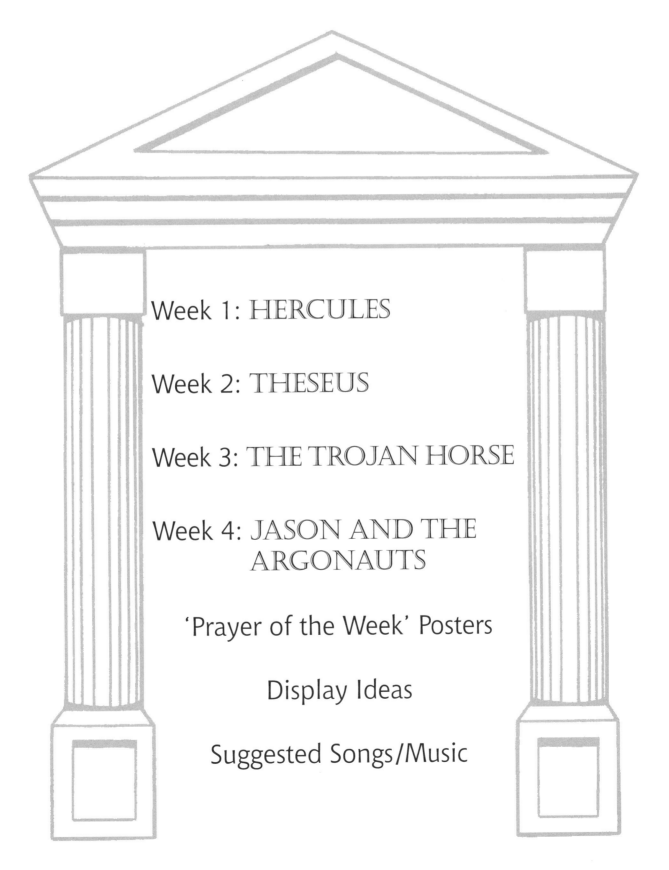

Week 1: HERCULES

Week 2: THESEUS

Week 3: THE TROJAN HORSE

Week 4: JASON AND THE ARGONAUTS

'Prayer of the Week' Posters

Display Ideas

Suggested Songs/Music

Week 1 of 4 – HERCULES

INTRODUCTION

The name Hercules has become synonymous with strength! Hercules is actually the Roman name for the Greek character Heracles – son of the god Zeus and Alcmene. Hera (the wife of Zeus) was understandably furious when Hercules was born – the result of her husband's infidelity – and she sent two great snakes to kill the baby. However, baby Hercules strangled the snakes. As a young man, Hercules killed a lion with his bare hands and wore its skin as a cloak and its head as a helmet!

However, life was not always easy for Hercules and in a bout of madness (sent on him by Hera) he killed his wife and children. In order to redeem himself, he was set 12 seemingly impossible tasks – which (driven on by the sorrow he felt at his terrible act) he somehow accomplished.

Hercules is a model of determination.

KEYS

Key idea:

One of the key points about Hercules was not that he was strong but that he used his strength. In the same way we need to use our God-given strengths, be they social, emotional, artistic or physical.

Key questions:
What are your key strengths?
Do you use them for good?
Do you ever misuse them?

Key challenge
Know and use your own strengths!

DAILY PRAYER

Lord,
like Hercules,
we face challenges in our lives.

Help us to realise that, with your help,
nothing is impossible.

AMEN.

ACTIVITY

Here are some of the 12 labours Hercules had to perform:

- killing the **Lion of Nemea** – which human-made weapons could not kill. Hercules hit it on the head, stunned it and then strangled it with his bare hands!

- killing the **nine-headed Hydra** – a fearsome beast whose snakes' heads breathed poison. One of the heads was immortal and if one head was chopped off, two grew back in its place! Hercules chopped off the eight mortal heads and used a torch to burn off the necks before new heads could develop. He then buried the ninth, immortal head.

- cleaning the **Augean stables** in a single day – quite some task, as these stables had housed thousands of cattle for 30 years without being cleaned! Hercules achieved this feat by diverting the course of two rivers so that they washed through the stables.

Notice how Hercules had to use **brains** as well as **brawn** to achieve success!

- Try to agree a rank order of difficulty!

- Now, try to think about modern-day labours in your lives. Think of people you know and any difficult situations that you've seen them deal with. In what way were they Herculean? What can you learn from them?

Week 2 of 4 – THESEUS

INTRODUCTION

The most famous story about Theseus concerns his adventure on the island of Crete. In order to appease the gods, seven young men and women were sent each year into an underground maze of tunnels, known as the Labyrinth. In the Labyrinth lived a fearsome monster called the Minotaur, which was half man and half bull. No one had ever returned from the Labyrinth.

Theseus though had a plan, thanks to the girl he loved, Ariadne – the daughter of the King of Crete. She gave him a large ball of string, one end of which he tied to the entrance to the Labyrinth. Then he unravelled it as he moved through the tunnels in search of the Minotaur. Needless to say, our hero, Theseus, overcame the Minotaur and found his way out by retracing his steps following the string.

He had many other adventures but will be most remembered for this occasion when brains were used to overcome brawn!

KEYS

Key idea

One of the key points about Theseus was that he needed to do more than just use his strength to solve the problem of the Labyrinth. He and Ariadne planned how he could overcome this challenge. We, in the same way, need to plan how to face challenges in our lives.

Key questions

Are you a good planner or do you just give knee-jerk reactions to problems you face?
Do you involve others in solving problems?
Do you ever involve God?

Key challenge

Think before you act!

DAILY PRAYER

**Lord, like Theseus, we are not always sure
where we are going in our lives.**

**Help us to realise that you are with us on our journey.
AMEN.**

ACTIVITY

Theseus and Ariadne planned how to overcome the problem of the Labyrinth. They used their combined brainpower. Use your brainpower together with some classmates to solve the following:

Challenge 1

Take four coins and arrange them so that there are two straight lines with three coins in each.

SOLUTION – for tutors only: put one coin on top of another, then use remaining coins to make 2 lines!

Challenge 2

Provide the next four letters in the following sequence:
J F M A M J J A

SOLUTION – for tutors only: S O N D (initials of months of the year).

Challenge 3

Three company directors called Jane, Jean and Joan meet to discuss a possible joint project. Each of them brings an assistant. They sit round a circular table and to ensure good communication no director sits next to her own assistant. Also, no two assistants sit next to each other. Jane sits to the right of Tim. Jean sits to Bill's left. Joan's assistant is called Graham. What is Jean's assistant called?

SOLUTION – for tutors only: Tim.

- Does it help to share ideas with others?
- Did you have to ask your tutor to help?
- Do you think it might be good on occasions to ask God's help when responding to life's challenges?

Week 3 of 4
THE TROJAN HORSE

INTRODUCTION

The legend of the Trojan Horse is believed to relate to an actual historical event in the twelfth century BC. The Spartans were laying siege to the city of Troy because of a conflict concerning Helen – a beautiful woman whose face was described as 'the face that launched a thousand ships'.

For 10 years, the Spartans tried to break the resolve of the Trojans and failed. But one day, the Trojans woke to see a huge wooden horse outside the city gates. Intrigued, the Trojans brought it inside the city walls and marvelled at it. However, unbeknown to them, the wooden horse was hollow and in it were hidden some crack Spartan troops.

When darkness fell, these troops came out of the horse and opened the city gates; the Spartan army flooded in, surprised the sleeping Trojans and won a great victory.

KEYS

Key idea

Problems can be solved but sometimes we need to think in different ways to solve them. While it is good to be persistent, it is also good to try thinking creatively about how to deal with problems we face.

Key questions

Do you solve problems creatively?
Do you ever try to look at things from other people's points of view?

Key challenge

Think of new ways to solve old problems.

DAILY PRAYER

Lord,
like the Spartans,
we too sometimes have long-standing problems.

Lord,
help us see that there can be an end to these
and help us to deal with them.
AMEN.

ACTIVITY

Let's consider the problem of conflicts in the world.

- Brainstorm a list of all the places in which there is conflict.
- What are the effects of such conflicts?

Conflicts cause terrible human suffering and we can't always see a way to solving big problems. However, we can 'think global and act local', i.e. deal with the conflicts in our own lives. If everyone dealt with their own conflicts better, perhaps as a global family we could sort out our differences.

How then can we solve them?
Have you ever thought about the following radical approaches?

- pray for the person who is causing you the problem!
- refuse to try to 'get back at someone' and in effect turn the other cheek!

Why not try it this week? If it's a long-standing problem, what have you got to lose?

Week 4 of 4
JASON AND THE ARGONAUTS

INTRODUCTION

Jason was the son of a king, but he had been sent away as a child because his father's brother had taken the throne and there were fears for Jason's safety. (Maybe you can think of someone else who, as a child, had to leave his country for safety.)

When Jason grew up he returned to Greece to claim the throne that was rightfully his. His uncle Pelias agreed to give him the throne, provided that he brought him the precious Golden Fleece which lay in a sacred grove in the far distant country of Colchis – under the eyes of a dragon that didn't sleep.

Jason got together a band of heroes and together they sailed in their ship – the Argos – in search of this trophy. After many adventures they achieved their goal. Jason returned and eventually regained the throne from the evil Pelias, who was killed by his two daughters.

KEYS

Key idea

One of the key points about Jason's quest was that he recognised and harnessed the talents of others – those who became the Argonauts. Together, they were strong and achieved their seemingly impossible goal.

Key questions

Do you recognise the strengths of others?
Are you good at working with others?
Does working with you help others to achieve?

Key challenge

Recognise the strengths of those around you!

DAILY PRAYER

Lord,
like Jason,
we are looking for things in our lives.

Help us to realise that,
with your help,
we can find those things which are truly important.
AMEN.

ACTIVITY

Jason, as a young man, had one basic objective in life – to regain the throne that was rightfully his. In order to achieve this objective he had to accomplish a particular task – namely, to find and recover the Golden Fleece.

Think today about your objectives in life.

What do you want to have accomplished in the next
- 5 years?
- 20 years?
- 50 years?

Talk together with a partner, in a group or as a class. Maybe you can find some common objectives.

Why not draw a road of life for yourself and put some milestones along the way (e.g. GCSEs, A-levels, degree, apprenticeship, first serious relationship, first book published, first car, first job, etc. – dream some attainable dreams!)

The first step on that road can be taken right now.

DISPLAY IDEA FOR 'GREEK MYTHOLOGY' THEME

Set aside some wall space and make a temple frontage. Display the prayers of the week and key ideas inside this frame. You could also bring in some Grecian-looking plant pots or urns to give the room a Greek 'feel'.

You could add relevant artefacts each week:

Week 1: HERCULES

Borrow a discus from the PE department
(a lot safer than a javelin!).

Week 2: THESEUS

Use a ball of string.

Week 3: THE TROJAN HORSE

Borrow a plastic shield from one of the children. They or their younger brothers and sisters may well have such things lying about at home. Alternatively, use a picture of a modern-day Helen – the face that launched a thousand ships!

Week 4: JASON AND THE ARGONAUTS

If you can get an old sheepskin rug, why not spray it gold? Alternatively use a bit of an old blanket – spray it and pass it off as the Golden Fleece. You might also be able to make a replica oar. You could ask pupils to bring in a team photo of their favourite football teams as examples of people working together like the Argonauts.

SUGGESTED SONGS/MUSIC FOR 'GREEK MYTHOLOGY' THEME

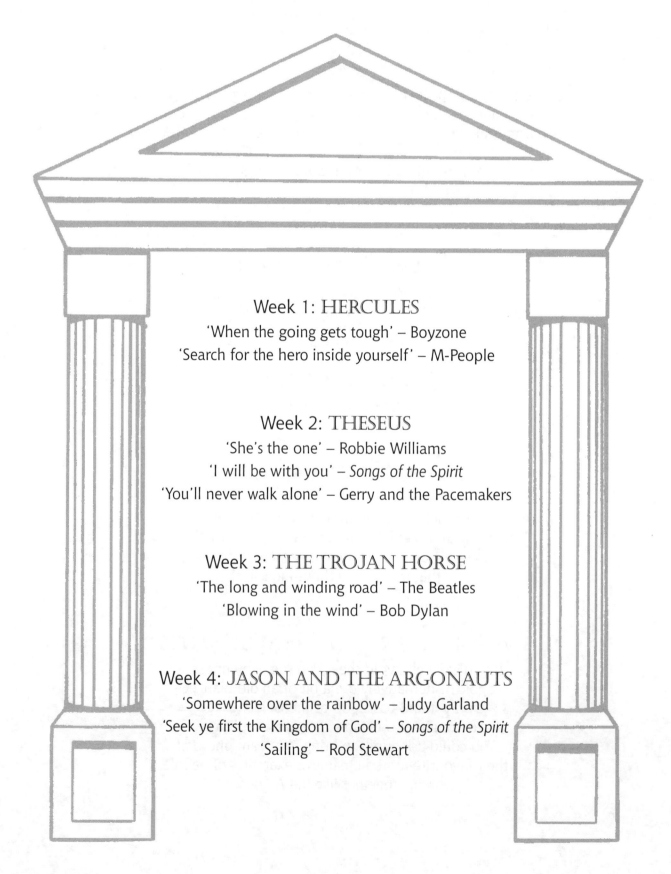

Week 1: HERCULES
'When the going gets tough' – Boyzone
'Search for the hero inside yourself' – M-People

Week 2: THESEUS
'She's the one' – Robbie Williams
'I will be with you' – *Songs of the Spirit*
'You'll never walk alone' – Gerry and the Pacemakers

Week 3: THE TROJAN HORSE
'The long and winding road' – The Beatles
'Blowing in the wind' – Bob Dylan

Week 4: JASON AND THE ARGONAUTS
'Somewhere over the rainbow' – Judy Garland
'Seek ye first the Kingdom of God' – *Songs of the Spirit*
'Sailing' – Rod Stewart

Week 1: HERCULES

DAILY PRAYER

Lord, like Hercules,
we face challenges in our lives.

Help us to realise that, with your help,
nothing is impossible.

AMEN.

Key idea

One of the key points about Hercules was
not that he was strong but that he used his
strength. In the same way we need to use
our God-given strengths, be they social,
emotional, artistic or physical.

Key questions

What are your key strengths?
Do you use them for good?
Do you ever misuse them?

Key challenge

Know and use your own strengths!

Week 2: THESEUS

DAILY PRAYER

Lord,
like Theseus, we are not always sure
where we are going in our lives.

Help us to realise that you are with
us on our journey.
AMEN.

Key idea

One of the key points about Theseus was that
he needed to do more than just use his strength
to solve the problem of the Labyrinth. He and
Ariadne planned how he could overcome this
challenge. We, in the same way, need to plan
how to face challenges in our lives.

Key questions

Are you a good planner or do you just give
knee-jerk reactions to problems you face?
Do you involve others in solving problems?
Do you ever involve God?

Key challenge

Think before you act!

Week 3:
THE TROJAN HORSE

DAILY PRAYER

Lord,
like the Spartans,
we too sometimes have long-standing problems.

Lord,
help us see that there can be an end to these
and help us to deal with them.
AMEN.

Key idea
Problems can be solved but sometimes we need to think in different ways to solve them. While it is good to be persistent, it is also good to try thinking creatively about how to deal with problems we face.

Key questions
Do you solve problems creatively? Do you ever try to look at things from other people's points of view?

Key challenge
Think of new ways to solve old problems.

Week 4:
JASON AND THE ARGONAUTS

DAILY PRAYER

Lord,
like Jason,
we are looking for things in our lives.

Help us to realise that,
with your help,
we can find those things which
are truly important.
AMEN.

Key idea

One of the key points about Jason's quest was
that he recognised and harnessed the talents
of others – those who became the Argonauts.
Together, they were strong and achieved
their seemingly impossible goal.

Key questions

Do you recognise the strengths of others?
Are you good at working with others?
Does working with you help others to achieve?

Key challenge

Recognise the strengths of those around you!

A three-week series based on

The X-Files
The Truth Is in You!

Week 1: Yeti and Nessie??

Week 2: Flying Saucers??

Week 3: The *Marie Celeste*??

'Prayer of the Week' Posters

Display Ideas

Suggested Songs/Music

Week 1 of 3

The X-Files – The Truth Is in You!

Yeti and Nessie?

Theme

One of the most popular TV programmes in recent years has been *The X-Files*. As we approached the end of the second millennium since the birth of Jesus, it seemed we were fascinated by things we couldn't really explain or prove – and still can't! Over the next few weeks we're going to look at some of these and ask: 'Is the truth out there in the world, or is truth something you experience for yourself on the inside?'

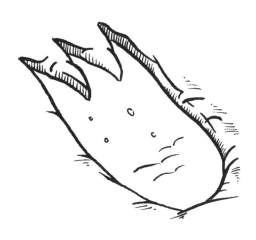

There have long been sightings of ape-like creatures. In the Himalayan mountain range the creature is referred to as the Abominable Snowman or the Yeti. It has been sighted by, among others, Sherpa Tensing Norgay, who accompanied Sir Edmund Hillary in the first conquest of Mount Everest. There have been many expeditions to try to find the Yeti, but all have failed to provide the conclusive evidence sceptics require. But what about you? How much proof do you need before you believe something? This week maybe you'll find out!

Would you believe it?

In 1938, off the coast of South Africa, a group of fishermen caught a fish of a type they'd never seen before. Eventually, some scientists found out that the fish was a species called the 'coelacanth', never before seen by humans. The coelacanth is dark brown in colour and grows to more than five feet in length, weighing more than ten stone. Unlike most fish, it gives birth to live young as opposed to laying eggs.

What was truly remarkable was that this species was thought to be extinct and could only be identified thanks to fossils dated as more than 300 million years old! So, a species which lived at the time of the dinosaurs is still alive today!

Would you have believed it?

Daily Prayer

Lord, it is so difficult to believe sometimes.
Help me to keep searching for the truth.
When I am ready, help me to make the leap of faith
that leads to knowing you.
Amen.

Activity

Which of the following is easy to prove?

• Dinosaurs existed.

• The Loch Ness Monster exists.

• You love someone.

• There is a place called America.

• There is a place called Heaven.

• Humans are evolved from apes.

• The earth is in orbit round the sun.

• A man called Jesus lived about 2,000 years ago
in an area which is now called Israel.

• The universe was created by a big explosion.

• There was something there before the universe existed.

• God made the world in seven days.

• God is important to some people when things go wrong.

Each of these points could prove a good starter for discussion.

Week 2 of 3

The X-Files – The Truth Is in You!

Flying Saucers?

Theme

For thousands of years, people have looked up at the stars and wondered at their beauty, but it is only relatively recently that we have become preoccupied with the question, 'Are we alone or is there life elsewhere in the universe?'

The phenomenon of Unidentified Flying Objects or flying saucers has been a common theme explored in twentieth century culture. The film *Close Encounters of the Third Kind* tells the story of one man's obsession with this idea. If you've seen *ET*, you'll know it concerns an encounter with extraterrestrials. The idea of alien abduction is often referred to in the programme *The X-Files*.

- So, are we alone?

- Will you have to see an alien to believe they exist?

- Will you have to see God before you believe?

Would you believe it?

- Between 1947 and 1969, the United States Air Force investigated 12,000 UFO sightings of which 701 remain unexplained!

- H. G. Wells wrote *The War of the Worlds* – a book about an alien invasion – in 1898, nearly a century before the film *Independence Day* was made!

- The cult of the UFO is such that in one Wigan paper there is a weekly column which records sightings over Wigan!

Would you believe it?

Daily prayer

Lord, it is so difficult to believe sometimes.
Help me to realise that you are always with me.
Amen.

Activity

The following is best delivered as a meditation, where pupils close their eyes and try to imagine the scene as it develops. Some gentle instrumental music in the background helps to set the right mood. Read through quite slowly, giving participants a chance to think.

Imagine you are in your room alone, late at night. You hear a sound outside and go out of the front door to investigate. You hear a whirring sound coming from above. You look up and see a flying saucer. It seems to be descending. The whirring sound gets louder and, as it draws nearer, you become aware of coloured lights on its under-side. Gently it descends and lands just a few yards away from you. The whirring sound stops.

A door opens and a radiant light shines out, making you shield your eyes. After a few seconds your eyes adjust and you are able to look into the light. Out steps a being. What does it look like? It approaches you and you feel at ease with it. You feel drawn towards it and soon you are standing opposite each other. You don't feel threatened. The creature greets you, saying it comes in peace. What does its voice sound like?

It says it can help you to achieve anything, as long as it is good not just for you, but for others too. It says it could help you to end hunger in the world; to bring healing to people; to make everyone equal. You think carefully. What do you ask for? The creature tells you that you can make a difference; that you can achieve your goal, but that you have to start small, with your friends and family, and that sometimes you may feel like you are achieving nothing. The creature says that if you talk to it in your mind when you feel down, you will be heard. It leaves with the words: 'I will be with you – even when you can't see me – I will be with you.' And in a sudden blinding flash of light the creature is gone and you are alone.

You go back to your room and know that life will never be the same again.

Week 3 of 3

The X-Files – The Truth Is in You!

The Marie Celeste?

Theme

On 5 November 1872, the American brig, the *Marie Celeste*, set sail from New York. A month and a day later it was spotted by the crew of the *Dei Gratia* sailing erratically in the Atlantic between the Azores and Portugal.

The *Dei Gratia* came alongside it and the crew boarded the *Marie Celeste*. The ship was deserted. The ship's log had last been filled in on 25 November, suggesting it had sailed without crew for nine days and had managed to travel 700 miles north-east in that time.

The crew's quarters were undamaged and the crew's belongings were all apparently there. The cargo was intact apart from a keg of alcohol, which appeared damaged. There was no evidence of a struggle but the ship's lifeboat was no longer on the ship.

What could have happened?

Would you believe it?

- The captain of the *Marie Celeste* had dinner the day before departure with the captain of the *Dei Gratia* – the very ship which found the *Marie Celeste* deserted in the vast expanse of the Atlantic Ocean.

- The *Marie Celeste* had originally been called the *Amazon* and its first captain had died within 48 hours of its launch.

- *Dei Gratia* means 'Thank God'.

Would you believe it?

Daily prayer

Lord, we never know what is going to happen in our lives.
Help us to live each moment knowing you are here with us.
Amen.

Activity

The story of the *Marie Celeste* has enthralled enthusiasts of the unexplained for over a century. All sorts of theories have been put forward to explain it. Here are some of those theories:

- the ship was attacked by a giant octopus-like creature called the Kraken

- the crew all got drunk and fell overboard

- the crew were abducted by aliens

- the ship was overcome by a freak storm and the crew was thrown overboard.

It would certainly make a great film. Your activity this week is to write a synopsis (summary of a story-line) to present to a Hollywood producer.

Those on board the ship were Captain Briggs, his wife and daughter and a crew of seven men. You can decide who you want to star in it and what characters they might play.

Yeti and Nessie??

Would you believe it?

↬ In 1938, off the coast of South Africa, a group of fishermen caught a fish of a type they'd never seen before. Eventually, some scientists found out that the fish was a species called the 'coelacanth', never before seen by humans.

↬ The coelacanth is dark brown in colour and grows to more than five feet in length, weighing more than ten stone. Unlike most fish, it gives birth to live young as opposed to laying eggs.

↬ What was truly remarkable was that this species was thought to be extinct and could only be identified thanks to fossils dated as more than 300 million years old! So, a species which lived at the time of the dinosaurs is still alive today!

Would you have believed it?

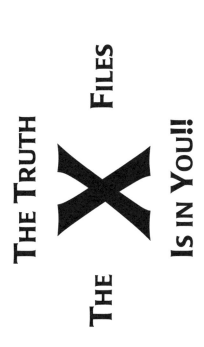

THE TRUTH

FILES

THE IS IN YOU!!

Daily Prayer

Lord, it is so difficult to believe sometimes.

Help me to keep searching for the truth.

When I am ready, help me to make the leap of faith that leads to knowing you.

Amen.

Flying Saucers??

Would you believe it?

- Between 1947 and 1969, the United States Air Force investigated 12,000 UFO sightings of which 701 remain unexplained!

- H. G. Wells wrote *The War of the Worlds* – a book about an alien invasion – in 1898, nearly a century before the film *Independence Day* was made!

- The cult of the UFO is such that in one Wigan paper there is a weekly column which records sightings over Wigan!

Would you believe it?

THE TRUTH

FILES

THE X IS IN YOU!!

Daily Prayer

Lord, it is so difficult to believe sometimes.

Help me to realise that you are always with me.

Amen.

The Marie Celeste ??

Would you believe it?

 The captain of the *Marie Celeste* had dinner the day before departure with the captain of the *Dei Gratia* – the very ship which found the *Marie Celeste* deserted in the vast expanse of the Atlantic Ocean.

 The *Marie Celeste* had originally been called the *Amazon* and its first captain had died within 48 hours of its launch.

 Dei Gratia means 'Thank God'.

Would you believe it?

THE TRUTH

THE X FILES

IS IN YOU!!

Daily Prayer

Lord, we never know what is going to happen in our lives.

Help us to live each moment knowing you are here with us.

Amen.

DISPLAY IDEA FOR 'THE X-FILES' THEME

Wall display: silver lettering mounted on black; dark-blue backing paper. Selection of *X-Files* posters and/or video cases.

The X-FILES

The Truth Is in You!

Week 1: Yeti and Nessie

Create a large footprint in 'snow': Make a template of a footprint and place it on a polystyrene tile or heavy-duty white card. Then spray glue around it and sprinkle polystyrene beads on glue. After a few sprayings and layers of beads this looks quite convincing.

Week 2: Flying Saucers

Make a flying saucer from cardboard. Cover it with aluminium foil or shiny paper and dangle it from the ceiling.

Week 3: The *Marie Celeste*

Place a table laid with a few pieces of crockery next to the wall. On the wall just above the table stick two triangular pieces of cloth to represent the sails of a ship.

SUGGESTED SONGS/MUSIC FOR 'THE X-FILES' THEME

Week 1: Yeti and Nessie

'The monster mash' – The Beach Boys
Jurassic Park theme – John Williams

Week 2: Flying Saucers

'You are not alone' – Michael Jackson
Close Encounters of the Third Kind theme – John Williams
ET theme – John Williams

Week 3: The *Marie Celeste*

'Sailing' – Rod Stewart

ADVENT ADVENTURE

AN ADVENT CALENDAR IN POSTERS AND WORDS

Illustrations by Paul Heesome

This series is based around 15 posters – one for each school day of the last three weeks of term. The idea is to create a sort of Advent Calendar by adding a poster to the wall each day.

With each poster is a 'thought for the day'. The teacher or a pupil could read this. (It would be best to give pupils a chance to practise how they would read it.) Alternatively, staff or pupils can give their own impression of the poster or event depicted in it.

A copy of the larger prayer used each day is provided for the wall.

ADVENT ADVENTURE 1 – Today's poster is entitled

Are you ready?

Thought for the day

The Advent term in schools is very often the time for the school's Open Night. Can you remember the last time you were preparing for Open Night?

Everyone is involved in some way, whether it is doing work for the displays, training to be a guide, practising dancing, playing and singing or even just keeping out of the teachers' way and getting on with work set.

So often, Open Night is a really successful event, and one of the main reasons for the success is the tremendous amount of preparation that goes into it. There's an old saying: 'If we fail to plan – we plan to fail!' It might sound corny but there's a ring of truth to it.

Advent is the time to plan for the coming of Jesus. But what do you plan for? Is it the giving of presents? Do you and your family plan for mega-meals and parties? These things are all fine and can be good, but if we lose the REASON for the SEASON – all of these are essentially fruitless and pointless.

So, this Advent, as we go through our Advent Adventure – let's wake up to the excitement of a new baby coming into our family. Let's wake up to the opportunities for building bridges that Christmas gives us. Let's wake up to get ready to put the Christ back into Christmas.

A few seconds of silent reflection

Daily prayer (said together):

Lord, we've walked in darkness too long.
We wait for the light of your love
to shine on us once more –
guiding, warming and protecting.
Lord, we wait for you! Amen.

1: Are you ready?

ADVENT ADVENTURE 2 – Today's poster is entitled

Prophets or profits?

Thought for the day

It is often thought that a prophet is someone who tells the future, but, in the Bible, the prophets do a great deal more than think and talk about the future. Generally, they looked back to the 'good old days' when all was well with God's Chosen People. Then they contrasted this with any bad things that were happening in their lifetime, reflecting that things weren't what they used to be. Only then did they consider the future – outlining how wonderful it would be when God's kingdom was fully established, but adding a warning as to what might happen if the people did not mend their ways.

So, prophets deal with the past, present and the future.

Christmas decorations up in October! Christmas cards with snow on! Christmas cards with robins on! Christmas cards with the Simpsons on! Pester the adults for your presents: Mobile phones! PCs! Furbies! Slade blaring out 'It's Chriiiiistmaaaaaaaas!' Turkey! Stuffing! Biggest bar of chocolate in the world! 'We wish you a merry Christmas!' Drink, drink, drink! Money, money, money! Buy, buy, buy! Profits! Profits! Profits!

What will your Christmas be about – PROPHETS or PROFITS?

A few seconds of silent reflection

Daily prayer (said together):

Lord, we've walked in darkness too long.
We wait for the light of your love
to shine on us once more –
guiding, warming and protecting.
Lord, we wait for you! Amen.

2: Prophets or profits?

ADVENT ADVENTURE 3 – Today's poster is entitled

Mary – Y9

Thought for the day

We tend to think of Mary, the mother of Jesus, as a radiant, beautiful lady – always smiling and ever patient. Artists over the centuries have tended to depict her as the epitome of perfection, with white and blue robes, a halo and a tendency to hover a few feet off the ground!

However, when you think about the reality that Mary faced, you start to realise what a tough time she went through. First of all, it's likely that Mary was only about 14 years old when the Angel Gabriel appeared to her. That's roughly the age of our Year 9 pupils. Not only did she have the shock and surprise of an angel appearing to her, she also had the task of explaining it all to her parents.

Can you imagine it? Mary comes down the stairs and says: 'Oh, Mum and Dad, I've got something to tell you.'
Mum replies, 'Oh, what's that, Mary?' Dad is not really listening – too busy reading the local news scroll!
    'I'm going to have a baby!'
    'You're what?!?!' Dad's listening now!
    'I'm going to have a baby.'
Now Dad's really angry: 'Who's the father – I'll kill him! Is it that Joseph?'
    'No, Dad, it's God himself by the power of the Holy Spirit.'
    'Have you been drinking?' Dad asks. 'I've never heard such nonsense in all my life! Who told you to say that?'
Mary replies, 'The Angel Gabriel, Dad . . . Dad? . . . Dad? . . .' But Dad does not reply because he's passed out.

Mary was one tough young girl who would have had to cope with village gossips and people laughing behind her back. Maybe we should remember her as a determined and resilient teenager, with the same sorts of feelings as teenagers today, who was chosen to do something really special for God. Is there something less spectacular that God has chosen for you?

A few seconds of silent reflection

Daily prayer (said together):

Lord, we've walked in darkness too long.
We wait for the light of your love
to shine on us once more –
guiding, warming and protecting.
Lord, we wait for you! Amen.

ADVENT ADVENTURE 4 – Today's poster is entitled

Angel!

Thought for the day

We heard yesterday how the Angel Gabriel appeared to the teenage Mary. But what do we know about angels? When you were younger, were you ever called 'a little angel'? It's the sort of thing doting parents, and particularly grandparents, say, isn't it?

What do *you* think of when you hear the word 'angel'? Is it chubby little babies draped with fine white silk, playing harps in the clouds? Is it androgynous beings, dressed in white, with enormous wings? What do angels look like?

The simple answer is that we don't know! But if we do a little detective work, we can say something about angels. If you look through the Bible, you'll find that almost every time an angel appears to an individual, the first words the angel says are: 'Don't be afraid!' If these are the first words, the logical conclusion to this is that angels must be absolutely terrifying!

So, we can guess that they must look frightening, but what is their purpose? Basically, they are messengers sent by God. They are biblical 'Kissograms' if you like. They pass on messages which are often surprising – surely none more so than the news that Mary was pregnant. They are also sent sometimes to protect and guide people.

Have you ever been an angel? Have you ever encouraged someone to believe in Jesus or are you too afraid to admit to others that you pray or believe? Have you ever looked after someone who needed help? You probably have – be that angel to someone today!

A few seconds of silent reflection

Daily prayer (said together):

Lord, we've walked in darkness too long.
We wait for the light of your love
to shine on us once more –
guiding, warming and protecting.
Lord, we wait for you! Amen.

4: Angel!

ADVENT ADVENTURE 5 – Today's poster is entitled

Emmanuel

Thought for the day

In the Gospel of Matthew, five prophecies are mentioned as being fulfilled by Jesus in the first two chapters. One of these is: 'A virgin shall conceive and give birth to a son – and he shall be called Emmanuel.'

The name 'Emmanuel' means 'God is with us'.

Have you ever had an Emmanuel moment when you've felt God close to you? If you have, it may have been during a time of trouble – a family difficulty or bereavement. Such moments are really precious and should be treasured.

There was once a man who had died and was looking back on his life as a journey with God. Through most of his life, he could see two sets of footprints in the sand and he said to God, 'I can see you were there with me – on my journey.' He noticed though that during the most rocky and difficult periods of his life, there was only one set of footprints and he said to God: 'Why did you abandon me when times were hard?' God answered: 'My son, when times were hard and you see only one set of footprints – that was when I carried you!'

You don't get Emmanuel moments just in church or at assemblies. They can happen any time, any place, anywhere. Give yourself a chance to experience God. Give yourself space; stop for just a few minutes when you get home tonight and let God carry you.

A few seconds of silent reflection

Daily prayer (said together):

Lord, we've walked in darkness too long.
We wait for the light of your love
to shine on us once more –
guiding, warming and protecting.
Lord, we wait for you! Amen.

5: Emmanuel

ADVENT ADVENTURE 6 – Today's poster is entitled

Joseph – forgotten hero!

Thought for the day

Joseph is the forgotten hero of the Christmas story. In the school nativity play he only gets to say, 'We are weary travellers – have you any room at your inn?'

In some school nativity plays even the sheep and cows get higher billing than Joseph! And yet, he was quite an amazing man.

Remember, he was engaged to Mary and she became pregnant. It is important to remember that, in those days, to be pregnant before you were married was considered scandalous. Joseph knew it was not his child, but he did not abandon Mary. When she told him it was God's child, he did not say she was round the twist. When the gossips were saying things about him and Mary, he stood by her.

When he and Mary were travelling to Bethlehem, you can appreciate that Mary – being heavily pregnant – would have got all the attention. When the wise men came to see Jesus, Joseph would not have been in the frame.

And yet, Joseph was the one who gave up his home and became a refugee with Mary and Jesus, in order to escape the massacre of the innocents at Bethlehem. Joseph was the one who worked as a carpenter to provide for Mary and Jesus – all the while knowing that Jesus was not his son. He would not have been human had he not had doubts at some times in his life about Mary's story of the Angel Gabriel. True, an angel did appear to Joseph in a dream – but would he have questioned this? How did he deal with all the doubts and upset he must have felt? Perhaps Joseph's theme song would have been 'Search for the hero inside yourself'.

Joseph – the forgotten hero who did find himself!

A few seconds of silent reflection

Daily prayer (said together):

Lord, we've walked in darkness too long.
We wait for the light of your love
to shine on us once more –
guiding, warming and protecting.
Lord, we wait for you! Amen.

6: Joseph – forgotten hero!

ADVENT ADVENTURE 7 – Today's poster is entitled

Census

Thought for the day

Every 10 years in Britain a nation-wide census takes place – the next census is due in 2001. The information gathered from it is essential in ensuring the country can plan for the future as regards the building of hospitals and schools. It helps government to plan for the training of a variety of essential professions. The first census in this country was in 1086, ordered by William the Conqueror – the result of it was *The Domesday Book.*

However, the Roman Empire had conducted surveys over a thousand years earlier. One of these was ordered by the Emperor Augustus (after whom, incidentally, the month of August is named) and the census was used by Roman officials to decide how much tax to levy on the people of the Empire. These surveys were far from popular. For a start each man had to go back, with his family, to his ancestors' home town. Where would you have to go?

In Joseph's case this meant a journey of over 100 miles, from Nazareth to Bethlehem. That is a considerable distance to have to walk, and you can imagine how awkward it would have been for the heavily pregnant Mary to make this journey. It would have taken four or five days – four or five days without even the basic home comforts; four or five days of carrying all they might need in case the baby was born; four or five days of either camping out or asking people to put them up (not a Little Chef or Trust House Forte in sight!); four or five days of wondering if their baby was going to be born on the road.

Many infant school nativity plays include the song 'Little donkey' but it doesn't really capture the discomfort, cold and fatigue that Mary and Joseph must have suffered. As we go through our Advent Adventure, let's remember that, for Joseph and Mary, it was not an exciting journey, but a stressful and exhausting one.

A few seconds of silent reflection

Daily prayer (said together):

Lord, we've walked in darkness too long.
We wait for the light of your love
to shine on us once more –
guiding, warming and protecting.
Lord, we wait for you! Amen.

ADVENT ADVENTURE 8 – Today's poster is entitled

Bethlehem

Thought for the day

The word 'Bethlehem' literally means 'house of bread', and it was here that the 'Bread of Life' – Jesus – was born. Even before the birth of Jesus, the town had great religious significance. It was the birthplace of the great Jewish leader, David. Indeed, Bethlehem became known as the town of David.

David was only a boy when God guided the prophet Samuel to him. His most famous exploit was the slaying of Goliath. At that time, battles were sometimes settled by letting the champions of the respective armies fight it out. The army whose champion won was then deemed to have won the battle. The enemies of the Israelites (David's people) were the Philistines. Their champion was Goliath – who was 9 feet 8 inches tall (that's about 3 feet taller than the basketball player, Michael Jordan). Not surprisingly, the Israelite king, Saul, had a few problems in finding anyone willing to take Goliath on. Eventually David volunteered. Saul gave David his own suit of armour, but the boy David, having put it on, found it so big and heavy that he couldn't walk, so he took it off and approached Goliath without armour or sword. When Goliath saw David, he started laughing – until a stone fired from David's sling hit him on the forehead, penetrated the skull and knocked him to the ground. David then picked up Goliath's sword and cut his head off.

David went on to become a great king. He was a gifted musician and wrote many songs, now recorded in the Bible in the book of Psalms. It is no surprise that the Israelites wanted another leader like David, and the prophets Isaiah and Micah said that this long-awaited Messiah would be born in Bethlehem. Bethlehem was and still is the focus of the Israelites' hope for the future.

Christians today sing the carol 'O little town of Bethlehem' and echo this sense of hope in the words:
The hopes and fears of all the years are met in thee tonight.

A few seconds of silent reflection

Daily prayer (said together):

Lord, we've walked in darkness too long.
We wait for the light of your love
to shine on us once more –
guiding, warming and protecting.
Lord, we wait for you! Amen.

8: Bethlehem

ADVENT ADVENTURE 9 – Today's poster is entitled

How many? How wise?

Thought for the day

Have you ever gone carol singing or had carol singers at your door? If you have, you will know the carol:

We three kings of Orient are;
bearing gifts we travel afar. . .

This is actually rather inaccurate. Firstly, the visitors from the East were probably astrologers rather than kings and, secondly, there is no mention in the Gospels of how many there were. It is a long-standing church tradition that there must have been three because three gifts were brought, and a mosaic created in the sixth century even named them as Balthazar, Melchior and Caspar. However, this is most likely inaccurate.

Were these astrologers – probably from the country we now call Iraq – the first century's answer to 'Dipstick Meg'? Nowadays, horoscopes are usually seen as a bit of fun, but at the time of these wise men, astrologers were well respected. They underwent years of training and some of the discoveries they made about the stars astound today's scientists.

Collectively they are also sometimes referred to as the Magi – from which we get the word 'magic'. So, what drove these educated men to follow a star? The desire to see the baby who would grow to be king was strong within them. They travelled hundreds of miles to meet Jesus.

Do you want to meet Jesus this Christmas?

A few seconds of silent reflection

Daily prayer (said together):

Lord, we've walked in darkness too long.
We wait for the light of your love
to shine on us once more –
guiding, warming and protecting.
Lord, we wait for you! Amen.

9: How many? How wise?

ADVENT ADVENTURE 10 – Today's poster is entitled

Ships of the desert

Thought for the day

Yesterday we heard about the wise men from the East. Let's spare a thought today for the beasts of burden which carried them and their entourage.

Known as 'ships of the desert', camels stand about six feet tall at the shoulders and can have either one or two humps, depending on the breed. Camels have the ability to go without water for several days. They can survive such hardship because they have special pouches in the stomach which can hold water to be released when required. Their humps are stores of flesh and fat, which means they can survive without food for long periods.

Camels are ideally adapted to travelling across desert landscapes. They have very long eyelashes, which protect their eyes in sandstorms. They also have the ability to close their nostrils. Camels have an acute sense of smell and can detect where water is. They are incredibly strong and can carry loads as big as 450 kilograms (1000 pounds/70-plus stone). They travel at a pace of about 2.5 miles per hour and can walk for up to 12 hours a day.

So what can we learn from camels? Sometimes we have to carry big burdens – emotional burdens – and we think there will never be an end to our problems. But we dig deep and somehow come through. Our lives are sometimes difficult journeys, but we are sustained by an inner strength, until we experience 'oasis moments' in our lives when we are refreshed by someone's act of kindness or love. And then the burden seems lighter and the journey easier.

Make it your challenge today to provide an 'oasis moment' for someone else.

A few seconds of silent reflection

Daily prayer (said together):

Lord, we've walked in darkness too long.
We wait for the light of your love
to shine on us once more –
guiding, warming and protecting.
Lord, we wait for you! Amen.

10: Ships of the desert

ADVENT ADVENTURE 11 – Today's poster is entitled

Star

Thought for the day

The wise men were said to have followed a star to Bethlehem. The idea of following a star is quite perplexing, because it is so far from our everyday experience – it sounds like something from *The X-Files*.

Many people have tried to find explanations for this star. These go from the plain wacky – such as, the star was an alien spacecraft – to the scientific – for example, the star was a visitation from Haley's Comet which orbits the earth every 76 years. However, it is difficult to reconcile such theories with Matthew's Gospel, which records that 'the star went forward and halted over the place where the child was.' Does a comet stop over a particular town? Maybe it was quite simply a miracle.

Another possible explanation lies in the way in which ancient writers reported the births of great historical figures. The birth of Julius Caesar, for example, was preceded by the appearance of a star, according to Roman writings. Similarly, it is recorded that a star appeared at the time of the birth of Alexander the Great. Could it be that the writer of Matthew's Gospel wanted to emphasise the importance of the birth of Jesus and so included the appearance of a celestial body? Such a literary device makes it clear that the birth of Jesus was an extraordinary event.

And this is the essence of the story of the birth of Jesus. Jesus was human like us and yet, at the same time, was the Son of God. The unexplained, mysterious star is just one aspect of the astounding story of his birth.

A few seconds of silent reflection

Daily prayer (said together):

Lord, we've walked in darkness too long.
We wait for the light of your love
to shine on us once more –
guiding, warming and protecting.
Lord, we wait for you! Amen.

ADVENT ADVENTURE 12 – Today's poster is entitled

Three gifts

Thought for the day

In England it has become a tradition for the Queen to offer gifts of gold, frankincense and myrrh at the altar of the Chapel Royal at St James' Palace, on the feast of the Epiphany.

But what are you planning to give this Christmas? For Christians, the emphasis should be on the giving of gifts, as we re-enact the giving of gifts by the wise men to Jesus. In some countries, Christmas gifts are exchanged on 6 January – the feast of the Epiphany. Would you be able to wait that long?

The gifts you get will tell us something about you. They may tell us that you support a certain football team, or like a particular pop group. They may tell us that you watch a certain TV programme, or like to choose your own clothes. So what of the gifts the wise men gave? What do they tell us about Jesus?

Firstly, gold: this was a gift traditionally given to kings. It emphasises that Jesus came to be a KING.

Secondly, frankincense: this is made from various gum resins, which, when burned, give off a strong fragrance. As the frankincense burns, the smoke rises and this is a symbol for Christians of their prayers rising to God. It emphasises Jesus' role as a PRIEST who was to lead people in prayer and towards God.

Finally, myrrh: again taken from the gum of certain trees. Myrrh was used as an oil for rubbing on the body, and was particularly used when people were close to death. A modern-day equivalent would be the oils used in aromatherapy. It emphasises that Jesus came to suffer and die like the PROPHETS before him.

JESUS – King, priest and prophet.

A few seconds of silent reflection

Daily prayer (said together):

Lord, we've walked in darkness too long.
We wait for the light of your love
to shine on us once more –
guiding, warming and protecting.
Lord, we wait for you! Amen.

12: Three gifts

ADVENT ADVENTURE 13 – Today's poster is entitled

Candle in the wind

Thought for the day

One of the most haunting aspects of the television coverage of Princess Diana's death was a report from outside Buckingham Palace, where people gathered one evening, holding lighted candles, and laying flowers at the Palace gates. The symbol of the candle continued with Elton John's reworking of the song 'Candle in the wind', originally written for Marilyn Monroe.

In the midst of a society where electricity lights our streets and homes, the symbolic power of the naked flickering flame of a candle is still immense.

For Christians, the lighted candle is a reminder that Jesus is the Light of the World – the one who guides us through the dark moments of life. As the new Church year starts, we light candles on Advent wreaths. Three of the candles are purple, a colour signifying the need to repent (turn over a new leaf) – and one is pink, as a sign of the joy we share at the birth of the baby Jesus.

When a child is baptised, a lighted candle is given to the parents as a reminder that Jesus should be the light which guides the child as it develops.

When a person dies, we often light votive candles for them. We look on the gently flickering flame, and somehow it helps us to pray.

This Christmas, try to take the opportunity to help someone who is having a bad time. Take the opportunity to pray for someone. Take the opportunity to . . .

. . . light a candle in the darkness.

A few seconds of silent reflection

Daily prayer (said together):

Lord, we've walked in darkness too long.
We wait for the light of your love
to shine on us once more –
guiding, warming and protecting.
Lord, we wait for you! Amen.

13: Candle in the wind

ADVENT ADVENTURE 14 – Today's poster is entitled

Shepherds

Thought for the day

The birth of Jesus is recorded in only two of the four Gospels – Matthew and Luke. In Matthew's account, the first people to visit Jesus are the Magi, or wise men. They bring rather grand gifts – gold, frankincense and myrrh.

In contrast, Luke records that the birth of Jesus is announced to shepherds out in the fields, looking after their sheep. This suggests that it was summer, and the shepherds had had to move further away from their usual grazing grounds to find food for their animals. It was quite usual for the shepherds to stay with the sheep in the fields when they were far from home.

You probably already know that shepherds were somewhat looked down upon at the time of Jesus. Jesus even made a bit of a joke about one in the parable of the Lost Sheep. It is significant, therefore, that the birth of the Messiah – the Son of God – was revealed to these poor shepherds. It is an indication that Jesus himself was to take an *option for the poor* – that he regarded all people as being *equal in dignity*.

This is a tremendous challenge for us. Maybe we can't make big dramatic gestures, like giving gold to the poor; but why not take the chance this Advent to do something for someone less fortunate than ourselves?

Feeding people's spirits is just as important as feeding their bodies – making them feel valued. Perhaps there is an old person living alone near you and this Christmas, with your parents' permission, you can make a visit and just chat with them and make them feel they are still valued in the community.

A few seconds of silent reflection

Daily prayer (said together):

Lord, we've walked in darkness too long.
We wait for the light of your love
to shine on us once more –
guiding, warming and protecting.
Lord, we wait for you! Amen.

14: Shepherds

ADVENT ADVENTURE 15 – Today's poster is entitled

New life!

Thought for the day

And so, we have reached the last day of our Advent Adventure in school. And we think about the birth of Jesus. As with every child, it was a miracle. As with every child, it brought great happiness. As with every child, there was sadness to follow at some point in his life.

But, for today, let's focus on the joy of new life. Forget about the nappies and sleepless nights. Think about the first smile, the first word, the first step!

And let's use it as a chance to start again ourselves. Let's throw off the cloaks of being 'cool', reserved and cold. Let's put on garments of joy, laughter and smiles. It may be cold over Christmas, but let's remember we are not God's frozen people – we are God's chosen people!

Let's enjoy the last day of school. If there are any relationships which need to be put right, take the chance to do it, so there's no chance for bitterness to develop over the holidays.

During the holidays, enjoy life and help others to enjoy it, too. We are celebrating one of the most momentous events in history – only Easter surpasses it, from the Christian point of view. So, celebrate – celebrate your friends, your family, your school – but above all, celebrate the birth of that baby, who cried aloud in a stable, some two thousand years ago, in a land far away.

Happy Christmas!

A few seconds of silent reflection

Daily prayer (said together):

Lord, we've walked in darkness too long.
We wait for the light of your love
to shine on us once more –
guiding, warming and protecting.
Lord, we wait for you! Amen.

15: New life!

Lord, we've walked in darkness too long.

We wait for the light of your love
to shine on us once more —
guiding, warming and protecting.

Lord, we wait for you!

Amen.

JESUS – THE LAST WEEK
IN POSTERS AND WORDS

This series is based around 15 posters – one for each school day of the last three weeks of term. The idea is to build up the notion of a journey through Jesus' last week by adding a poster to the wall each day.

With each poster is a 'thought for the day'. This could be read by the teacher or a pupil. (It would be best to give pupils a chance to practise how they would read it.) Alternatively, staff or pupils can give their own impression of the poster or event depicted in it.

The prayer to be used each day of the journey was written by Desmond Tutu. A copy for the wall is provided.

1 JESUS – THE HERO!

THOUGHT FOR THE DAY

Has your local football team ever won anything? Even if they haven't, you will have seen football teams going back to their home towns the day after winning the FA Cup. Thousands of people wear the team's strip. They wave flags and scarves. They chant the names of the players and sing songs of triumph!

The last week of Jesus' life also started in triumph. He was welcomed into Jerusalem by people who really thought he was someone special. They had heard how he had helped people and performed miracles, and they wanted him to use his power to set them free from the Romans, who had occupied Israel. They wanted Jesus to use his powers for them.

Maybe we, too, fall into the same trap of expecting Jesus to do things for us. Maybe we think that if we pray, everything will go all right for us in life, that we'll pass our exams, get good jobs and live happily ever after. Life is rarely that simple!

Perhaps we should think less about what Jesus can do for us – and more about what we can do for others. That's being a hero!

JESUS – THE HERO!

A FEW SECONDS OF SILENT REFLECTION

PRAYER

Good is stronger than evil.
Love is stronger than hate.
Light is stronger than darkness.
Life is stronger than death.
Victory is ours –
through him who loves us.
Amen.

Desmond Tutu

1 JESUS – THE HERO!

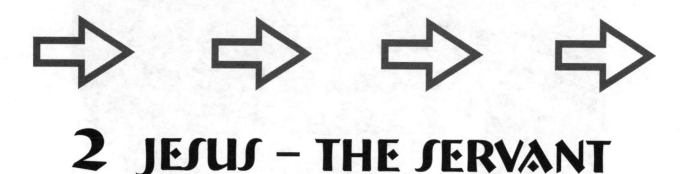

2 JESUS – THE SERVANT

THOUGHT FOR THE DAY

Jesus washes his friends' feet

Are you a selfish person? The answer will probably be, 'No – of course not!'

However, maybe there is one area of your life where you are a bit selfish. Maybe you expect your mum to tidy your room. Maybe you expect to get whatever you want for your birthday. Maybe you expect your tea to be cooked for you. Maybe you expect your clothes to be washed and ironed for you.

Today, we think about how Jesus showed us that it was important to care for others in the really practical things of life. He – the leader – washed the feet of his disciples, to show that we should not expect to be waited on hand and foot, but that we should do what we can to make life better for others.

Maybe that could be your challenge for today – to DO something for someone else that you don't normally do.

JESUS – THE SERVANT

A FEW SECONDS OF SILENT REFLECTION

PRAYER

Good is stronger than evil.
Love is stronger than hate.
Light is stronger than darkness.
Life is stronger than death.
Victory is ours –
through him who loves us.
Amen.

Desmond Tutu

2 JESUS – THE SERVANT

3 JESUS – ALONE

THOUGHT FOR THE DAY

Jesus prays in the Garden of Gethsemane, while his disciples sleep

Have you ever been 'stood up' – arranged to meet someone and they've not turned up? Have you ever been let down by someone who promised to do something for you, or who promised to support you in some way but didn't?

Imagine how Jesus felt when he asked his friends to pray for him. They had seen him perform miracles. They had seen him walk on water. And yet, they fell asleep. It is easy to feel sympathy for Peter, James and John. After all, it was late – and they had just had a good meal and drunk some wine. Nevertheless – they let Jesus down – even though they didn't mean to.

Maybe you could make a special effort not to let anyone down in any way today. Maybe you could make a special effort today to include someone in your group who seems a bit lonely.

JESUS – ALONE

A FEW SECONDS OF SILENT REFLECTION

PRAYER

Good is stronger than evil.
Love is stronger than hate.
Light is stronger than darkness.
Life is stronger than death.
Victory is ours –
through him who loves us.
Amen.

Desmond Tutu

3 JESUS – ALONE

4 JESUS – I DON'T KNOW HIM!

THOUGHT FOR THE DAY

Peter denies Jesus three times

This is one of the most famous stories in the Gospels. Peter pretends that he doesn't know Jesus. Basically, he lies – three times. The very fact that it was three times suggests that it was no mistake. When Peter said he didn't know Jesus the first time, it was to a servant girl. Then, when others asked him about it, he had to continue the lie until, finally, he had to shout that he didn't know Jesus.

Lying gets out of hand very easily. It can start with saying we have forgotten our homework, when really we haven't done it. It can move on to saying that your mum is writing you a note about it. It can continue with saying that your Year Manager wants to see you, when you are supposed to be at break-time detention, and so on.

Maybe today we can all resolve to speak the truth, even if it means we get into trouble.

JESUS – I DON'T KNOW HIM!

A FEW SECONDS OF SILENT REFLECTION

PRAYER

Good is stronger than evil.
Love is stronger than hate.
Light is stronger than darkness.
Life is stronger than death.
Victory is ours –
through him who loves us.
Amen.

Desmond Tutu

4 JESUS –
I DON'T KNOW HIM!

5 JESUS – WE DON'T WANT HIM!

THOUGHT FOR THE DAY

The crowd shout for Barabbas to be freed

Does your class or group of friends sometimes deliberately exclude someone and make life unhappy for them? Sometimes it starts because someone is given a nickname and everyone latches onto it and uses it abusively. It's often done in a sly, snide way, which undermines a person's confidence. The victim feels 'got at', left out and their self-esteem hits rock bottom.

Can you imagine how Jesus must have felt when the crowd chose to have Pilate free Barabbas – a murderer – instead of him? Surely some of these people were the same ones who had acclaimed him a hero when he came into Jerusalem. But they had been 'got at' by the chief priests and were too afraid to go against them.

Maybe your challenge could be to stand up for a victim next time you see someone being verbally or emotionally bullied.

JESUS – WE DON'T WANT HIM!

A FEW SECONDS OF SILENT REFLECTION

PRAYER

Good is stronger than evil.
Love is stronger than hate.
Light is stronger than darkness.
Life is stronger than death.
Victory is ours –
through him who loves us.
Amen.

Desmond Tutu

5 JESUS –
WE DON'T WANT HIM!

6 JESUS – NOTHING TO DO WITH ME

THOUGHT FOR THE DAY

Jesus before Pilate, who washes his hands

There is a series of adverts on the TV for Special Constables. One of them involves a group of youngsters roughing up a schoolboy in uniform. Most people just walk on by – they're too frightened to get involved.

In the same way, Pilate had the power to prevent Jesus being crucified, but he did literally 'wash his hands', as if that meant he wouldn't get the blame. However, the story of Pilate is still known and he is blamed 2,000 years later for allowing Jesus to die.

There are situations where we can step in and stop something wrong happening, and today we are challenged to do that. A simple way to do this is to think of the Third World. It's easy to say, 'It's nothing to do with me', but we shouldn't. Why not think about how you can help raise some money for CAFOD or some other charity this week, to show that you are not 'washing your hands' of the responsibility for those who suffer?

JESUS – NOTHING TO DO WITH ME

A FEW SECONDS OF SILENT REFLECTION

PRAYER

Good is stronger than evil.
Love is stronger than hate.
Light is stronger than darkness.
Life is stronger than death.
Victory is ours –
through him who loves us.
Amen.

Desmond Tutu

6 JESUS –
NOTHING TO DO WITH ME

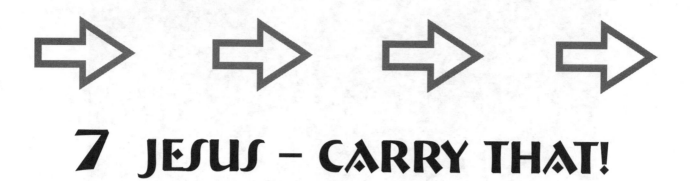

7 JESUS – CARRY THAT!

THOUGHT FOR THE DAY

Jesus receives the cross

We have all got something in our lives that weighs us down. It may be a health problem, a relationship problem, a death in the family, a dissatisfaction with our appearance or weight, worries over money, concerns over what our parents expect of us, and so on. These can all be difficult crosses to bear.

Jesus had to carry a large wooden cross-beam. The traditional image of Jesus carrying a full cross is probably incorrect, as it was customary at that time to have the vertical part of a cross fixed permanently into the ground. The cross-beam would then be hauled up the vertical part to form the cross shape.

Jesus had to accept something that wasn't fair. It wasn't fair that he should be given the cross. It's not fair that some people have more difficult crosses to bear than others. Maybe today's challenge could be to make sure we don't add to anyone's cross by what we say, or do or don't do.

JESUS – CARRY THAT!

A FEW SECONDS OF SILENT REFLECTION

PRAYER

Good is stronger than evil.
Love is stronger than hate.
Light is stronger than darkness.
Life is stronger than death.
Victory is ours –
through him who loves us.
Amen.

Desmond Tutu

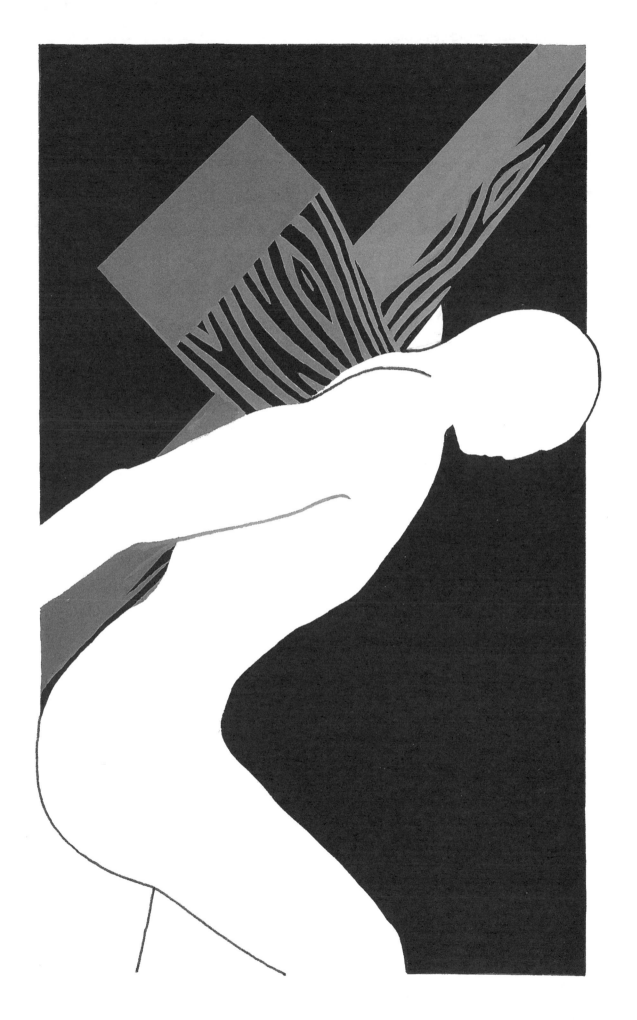

7 JESUS – CARRY THAT!

8 JESUS – THE WEAKLING

THOUGHT FOR THE DAY

Simon of Cyrene carries the cross of Jesus

Jesus became so weak that the soldiers were afraid he was going to die before he could be crucified. So they grabbed Simon of Cyrene out of the crowd and made him carry the cross-beam for Jesus. Maybe you didn't realise that this was probably a case of racial discrimination, because Simon of Cyrene was almost certainly black. The soldiers picked him – an African – out of the crowd and forced him to help Jesus.

Simon probably didn't see it as an honour to help Jesus. As a stranger in Jerusalem, he wouldn't have known what was going on. And yet his name has been remembered for 2,000 years. While he didn't see it as an honour to help Jesus at the time, it seems that this experience had a profound effect on Simon – so much so that his name was written in the Gospels, which were written more than 30 years later.

Sometimes, when we're asked to help others in some way, we resent it – maybe we throw a strop when asked to go to the shops or clean our room. Our challenge today is to help others willingly.

JESUS – THE WEAKLING

A FEW SECONDS OF SILENT REFLECTION

PRAYER

Good is stronger than evil.
Love is stronger than hate.
Light is stronger than darkness.
Life is stronger than death.
Victory is ours –
through him who loves us.
Amen.

Desmond Tutu

8 JESUS – THE WEAKLING

9 JESUS – THE FACE

THOUGHT FOR THE DAY

Veronica wipes the face of Jesus

Although there is no mention of it in the Gospels, there is a Church tradition that Veronica was so overcome to see Jesus suffering that she burst through the line of soldiers escorting him and wiped the face of Jesus on his journey to Golgotha. This tradition suggests that a full photographic imprint of the face of Jesus was left on the cloth used.

Have you ever wondered what Jesus must have looked like? European Christians tend to think of Jesus as being tall, slim, and white, with long straight hair, a beard and piercing eyes. African Christians picture Jesus as a black man. Chinese Christians think of Jesus as having oriental features.

Today, though, think to yourself – 'Has Jesus made any impression on my life?' If not, perhaps you need to think about how you can help Jesus, like Veronica did. Of course, you can't help Jesus directly, but maybe you can help someone else. In helping them – you are helping Jesus.

JESUS – THE FACE

A FEW SECONDS OF SILENT REFLECTION

PRAYER

Good is stronger than evil.
Love is stronger than hate.
Light is stronger than darkness.
Life is stronger than death.
Victory is ours –
through him who loves us.
Amen.

Desmond Tutu

9 JESUS – THE FACE

10 JESUS – CRUCIFIED!

THOUGHT FOR THE DAY

Having reached Golgotha ('the Place of the Skull'), Jesus was nailed to the cross. The crude nails used would have been about six inches long and would almost certainly have been hammered in through the wrist and not the palm of the hand. A nail driven through the palm would have ripped through the hand tissue and would not keep the victim on the cross.

As the nails were driven in, Jesus said: 'Father – forgive them – they don't know what they're doing.'

This gives some idea of how deeply Jesus loved everyone. There is a story about a Roman soldier who met Jesus. The soldier asked, 'You talk about loving enemies as well as friends. Well, I am a soldier who oppresses your people – who despises your Jewish religion. How much do you love me?'

And Jesus replied: 'This much!' And he stretched out his arms and they nailed him to the cross.

JESUS – CRUCIFIED!

A FEW SECONDS OF SILENT REFLECTION

PRAYER

Good is stronger than evil.
Love is stronger than hate.
Light is stronger than darkness.
Life is stronger than death.
Victory is ours –
through him who loves us.
Amen.

Desmond Tutu

10 JESUS – CRUCIFIED!

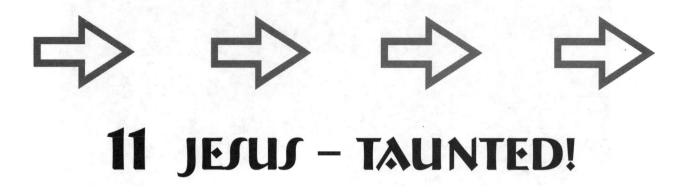

11 JESUS – TAUNTED!

THOUGHT FOR THE DAY

Have you ever had anyone rub it in when you've done something daft? Have you ever had someone really put the boot in when you're already feeling rotten? Maybe you've made someone else feel bad by what you've said, by verbally abusing them.

Charles Dickens once said: 'There is a great man who makes others feel small, but the really great man is the one who makes other people feel big.' Sometimes we use our mouths to belittle others – to make them feel small or soft or useless.

Even when Jesus was on the cross, three groups of people taunted him. They were the chief priests (religious people), the soldiers and the passers-by. He was dying, but they couldn't resist the temptation to have a laugh at Jesus.

Today's challenge is for us to resist the temptation to skit or belittle others.

JESUS – TAUNTED!

A FEW SECONDS OF SILENT REFLECTION

PRAYER

Good is stronger than evil.
Love is stronger than hate.
Light is stronger than darkness.
Life is stronger than death.
Victory is ours –
through him who loves us.
Amen.

Desmond Tutu

11 JESUS – TAUNTED!

12 JESUS – DEAD!

THOUGHT FOR THE DAY

Finally, after six hours on the cross, Jesus cried out: 'Eloi, eloi, lama sabachtani?' which means 'My God, my God, why have you abandoned me?'

Many people think that this was Jesus in despair – thinking that God had given up on him. However, these words are the first words of Psalm 22, which was a song describing how Yahweh (the Jewish name for God) would save all who were suffering, and change the world into a better place. It is a song of triumph.

So, Jesus' final words are not a cry of despair. Jesus was singing a song of victory.

JESUS – DEAD!

A FEW SECONDS OF SILENT REFLECTION

PRAYER

Good is stronger than evil.
Love is stronger than hate.
Light is stronger than darkness.
Life is stronger than death.
Victory is ours –
through him who loves us.
Amen.

Desmond Tutu

12 JESUS – DEAD!

13 JESUS – BURIED

THOUGHT FOR THE DAY

Jesus is placed in the tomb

We all have had bad things happen to us, things we prefer not to think about. We try to put them at the back of our minds and forget about them. But every now and again the memories flood back and we relive the experience.

Imagine how the followers of Jesus felt as his body was taken from the cross and put in the tomb. They must have thought that their great adventure with Jesus was over. They must have thought it was all pretty pointless and perhaps wanted to put it out of their minds. It was not a time for rejoicing – or celebrating. It was a time for sadness. Maybe some of them (like Peter) were thinking about what they wanted to say to Jesus before he died. Maybe they felt guilty about running away. Maybe they were saying to themselves: 'If only I'd stood by him'; 'If only I'd stayed awake in the Garden, I could have warned him'; 'If only I'd carried his cross for him'; 'If only I'd . . . '

Why not take the chance today to do something you should have done, or say something you should have said – so that you won't have to say, 'If only I'd . . . '

JESUS – BURIED

**A FEW
SECONDS OF SILENT
REFLECTION**

PRAYER

Good is stronger than evil.
Love is stronger than hate.
Light is stronger than darkness.
Life is stronger than death.
Victory is ours –
through him who loves us.
Amen.

Desmond Tutu

13 JESUS – BURIED

14 JESUS – WHERE IS HE?

THOUGHT FOR THE DAY

The empty tomb

Have you ever watched *The X-Files*? They can be really scary in an exciting sort of way. Have you ever been somewhere really spooky – where you're almost too scared to stay but too frightened to move on? Have you ever had the experience of being in a little world of your own, when someone walks in and gives you a tremendous shock that makes your heart pound?

The women who went to Jesus' tomb, very early on the Sunday morning after he'd been buried, had just such an experience. It would have been a bit dark and cold, because it was very early. They (we're not sure whether there were two or three of them – the Gospels don't agree) were walking through a graveyard. No one else would have been around. As they approached the tomb, they saw the stone covering the entrance had been rolled away. What would you have done? Would you have walked in? Would you have said: 'After you, Mary'? Would you have been frightened?

Anyway, the women did go in (according to Luke), and Jesus' body had gone.

And then – out of nowhere – two men appeared. Can you imagine how the women would have jumped? The men told them that Jesus had risen from the dead. Would you have believed them?

JESUS – WHERE IS HE?

A FEW SECONDS OF SILENT REFLECTION

PRAYER

Good is stronger than evil.
Love is stronger than hate.
Light is stronger than darkness.
Life is stronger than death.
Victory is ours –
through him who loves us.
Amen.

Desmond Tutu

14 JESUS – WHERE IS HE?

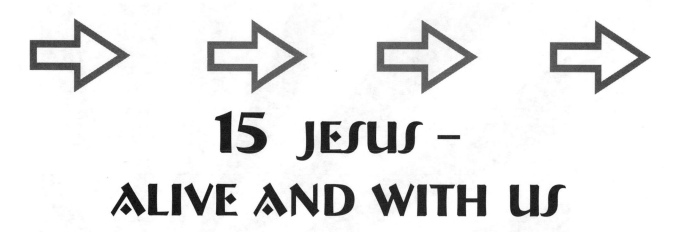

15 JESUS – ALIVE AND WITH US

THOUGHT FOR THE DAY

Jesus appears to the disciples but they do not recognise him

Have you ever met someone whose face you recognise, but you can't quite place them? As you get older it seems to happen more and more! After you've left school, you'll see your ex-teachers in town and maybe say 'Hello' to them – and be faced with a rather glazed look and furrowed brow as they try to dig up your name from their memory banks.

The Gospels tell slightly different stories about what happened after Jesus rose from the dead, but one fairly common feature of these stories is that his followers do not recognise him immediately. Was that because they were not expecting to see him? Was it because he had changed in some way? We don't really know.

What does happen, though, is that they recognise Jesus in his actions and words. We too should not expect to see Jesus face to face. Would we recognise him anyway? However, we can meet Jesus whenever someone does something that Jesus would have done. We meet Jesus in acts of kindness – in words of justice and peace – we meet Jesus in each other, when we do what Jesus would have done.

Try to see the risen Jesus in someone else today. And look in the mirror and see if you are sometimes Jesus to someone else – through what you say and do.

Enjoy your Easter Holidays!

JESUS – ALIVE AND WITH US

A FEW SECONDS OF SILENT REFLECTION

PRAYER

Good is stronger than evil.
Love is stronger than hate.
Light is stronger than darkness.
Life is stronger than death.
Victory is ours –
through him who loves us.
Amen.

Desmond Tutu

15 JESUS –
ALIVE AND WITH US

PRAYER

Good is stronger than evil.

Love is stronger than hate.

Light is stronger than darkness.

Life is stronger than death.

Victory is ours —

through him who loves us.

Amen.

Desmond Tutu